PARENTING AN AUTISTIC CHILD

A GUIDE TO UNDERSTANDING THE ASD DIAGNOSIS AND YOUR CHILD'S NEW NORMAL TO HELP THEM THRIVE

ISABELLA M. FIORI

TABLE OF CONTENTS

INTRODUCTION

For many parents, the start of their experience with an autistic child goes like this: You wonder why your child is developing slower than usual for their age, so you take them to a doctor. Sometimes, the "problem" is caught immediately; other times, it requires more digging. You take your child home and wonder what the issue could be, frantically Googling symptoms to see if anything will point you in the right direction. Over and over, webpages keep bringing you to a common consideration—autism. But your child cannot be autistic… Can they?

Autism spectrum disorder (ASD) can be confusing and scary, especially if you do not know what to expect. Your child might have just been diagnosed, or they may have had a diagnosis for a while. Everything from the doctor's visits to the "what now" questions can burden your mind—what are you supposed to do with this information? How will you help your child when you have more questions than answers?

There are likely many other things rattling around in your head right now. This sense of uncertainty leaves you struggling and wondering where to begin. You might think that you did something wrong that caused your child's autism, or you may feel like they will never be able to succeed in a world that was not built for them. You may ask why your child is being punished. These are entirely typical questions and concerns, many of which I had myself at the beginning of my journey of parenting a child with ASD.

You are not alone. As the mother of an autistic little girl, I have dealt with the ins and outs of parenting a child with autism. I want to help people like you navigate the same painful time. Trust me—I felt lost and helpless when my daughter was diagnosed, but now that it has been a few years, I feel capable of helping others in the same situation I was. As a mother of a child with ASD, I will stop at nothing to ensure she has all the resources and help she needs. I want you to be able to do the same for your child!

This book will answer most questions you may have about ASD. Throughout this book, you will gain many resources to help yourself and your little one navigate this upsetting time. You'll uncover the secrets to helping your child thrive, empowering you as a parent and them as a child to handle anything that comes your way.

I will help guide you every step of the way. Nothing compares to the love a parent has for their child, and I know that you have what it takes to support your child right now—you just need a little guidance. Without further ado, let's get started.

1

WHAT IS AUTISM?

As a parent of a child with autism, many questions must be running through your mind. What is autism? What are the common signs? I've been checking my child for signs and missed them. Why is everything so confusing right now? Why is it so difficult to get a diagnosis? These are some common questions for parents of children with autism—or suspected autism—and all of them, and more will be answered. Do not worry—you are on your way to finding out what autism is and the context surrounding it, allowing you to understand your child much better.

WHAT IS AUTISM?

The first thing you must understand about autism is that it is not an illness. I'll repeat it because it is so important to understand: Autism is not an illness! This is a common misconception. If it is something you previously thought, do not worry; many people believe this too, but that is why you are here: to get the correct information to become more informed, making it easier for you to understand and help your child.

So, if autism is not an illness, what is it? Rather than an illness, autism is a spectrum disorder, which is why it's also called ASD (Autism Spectrum Disorder). In other words, ASD falls on a broad spectrum, and an individual can fall anywhere within that spectrum. This means that autism isn't just about having it or not. Autism presents itself in different forms and is categorized by doctors on a scale from 1-3, with level 1 requiring a lower level of support and level 3 requiring a higher level of support.

I suppose that still does not tell you much about what autism is. Autism is a neurodevelopmental disability, and it falls under the neurodivergent umbrella, which primarily impacts brain function. There are two main ways to explain brain functions- neurodiversity and neurotypical. Neurodiversity is a term used to describe how the human brain works. The idea is that there's no "correct" way for how the brain works. Instead, people perceive and respond to the world in various courses, and these differences are to be embraced and encouraged (Child Mind Institute, 2023). Neurotypical refers to people with similar brain functions to most of their peers; they develop skills around the same rate as others their age. People with autism function with higher or lower mental capacity depending on the subject, topic, or concept. For instance, one autistic child might be better at logical pursuits, while another autistic child might be better at abstract thinking and creativity. People experience the disorder differently, which is why it is on a spectrum. The neurodivergent umbrella, on the other hand, is, as the name suggests—an umbrella term for the neurological brain characteristics that present in people with disorders such as ADHD, Autism, Anxiety, Dyslexia, Dyspraxia, Depression, OCD, PTSD, Tic disorders, and many others.

It is also essential to understand that ASD is the name given to a broad range of conditions, and a combination of some conditions makes someone autistic. For example, a child with autism can have a speech delay; a neurotypical child can also have a speech delay. The speech delay is not what makes a child autistic; it is the combination of a speech delay with other conditions that would create challenges in social skills, repetitive behaviors, etc., that would make the child autistic.

An ASD diagnosis is based on several things. Primarily, a diagnosis is based on observable characteristics and behavior. Unlike seizures or other medical conditions, no medical tests can diagnose autism; it is not as simple as an EEG, a blood draw, a CT scan, or an MRI. Instead, during an ASD diagnosis, a professional must examine your child for various characteristics that may or may not indicate ASD. This is what makes getting a diagnosis for ASD so hard, no matter the age or gender. Some people do not seem to be autistic at all based on what little testing is available, which makes it possible for professionals to overlook a potential case of ASD. This was the case with my daughter; she was prescreened for autism by her pediatrician at six months, 12 months, and 18 months. Although we raised some concerns regarding ASD, her pediatrician immediately shut them down because "a child with such a strong bond with her parents can't be autistic."

It is of paramount importance for parents and professionals to understand that not everyone who experiences ASD will have the same behaviors. For example, some people with ASD tend to rock back and forth or "flap" their hands—motions referred to as stimming, which help them process their emotions. But this does not look the same for everybody, nor is it something that everyone with ASD experiences. This is another reason why professionals can struggle to provide a diagnosis. This is even more complicated because not all autistic people have all the signs of ASD, and some people display "autistic characteristics" like stimming without being autistic. As you can probably tell, ASD is a rather complex disorder; if you are frustrated or confused, you are not alone. I had trouble understanding my daughter's diagnosis even though I had some previous understanding of ASD. My goddaughter was diagnosed with ASD while I was pregnant. I tried to learn as much as I could about the disorder. I knew the main things to look for in a child with autism. Not making eye contact, not answering when their name is called, not being social, not liking to cuddle, not forming strong bonds with others, etc. These are generalizations; not all children will display these so-called "most common characteristics." My daughter did not show any of these characteristics. And even though there was a child I was close to with ASD, my own child's ASD blinded me. My goddaughter and daughter have very different characteristics of ASD. I would watch my daughter closely, looking for some of the "most common characteristics," I would also observe to see if she displayed any of the characteristics displayed by my goddaughter; I didn't see many similarities, so I concluded that the pediatrician was correct. His assurance gave me a sense of relief. I would tell myself, "My husband is probably exaggerating the characteristics displayed by our daughter." At one point, he also thought he was looking too much into it. After all, all kids fidget and have unique quirks; more on that later. For now, let's look at the autism timeline.

AUTISM TIMELINE

The history of autism goes very far back. Many people also believe in the misconception that autism is a new disorder. Autism has decades of research and study behind it, which is exciting and vital to be aware of. According to most sources, the timeline of the history of ASD looks something like this (The Recovery Village, 2022):

- In 1908, German psychiatrist Eugene Bleuler created the term "autism," originally used to describe especially severe cases of schizophrenia. This condition was initially described as one involving retreating to one's inner world to avoid facing the cruel realities of the real world.
- In 1943, a child psychiatrist for Johns Hopkins University named Leo Kanner determined that

autism was distinct—at least in children. Kanner described it as infantile autism, and the key symptoms were obsessiveness, difficulty socializing, and needing everything to be the same.

- In 1944, just a year later, a pediatrician at the University of Vienna named Hans Asperger described something he called "autistic psychopathy," which held similar traits to Kanner's infantile autism. Asperger studied those who have something called "high functioning autism," primarily, which is a label the community is trying to break away from. A particular set of autistic characteristics came to be known as Asperger's syndrome, which is something else the autistic community is leaving in the dust—and something I'll talk about more in the next section.

- We take quite a jump to our subsequent historical development regarding autism, revisiting Kanner. In 1967, Kanner and other psychologists developed the theory that autism was the result of emotionally cold mothers and poor parenting in early childhood. Kanner surmised that many symptoms of autism were a result of this type of parenting. Bruno Bettelheim supported this theory and popularized it in the years to come. We now know that autism is not the result of "bad parenting," another common misconception surrounding the disorder.

- In 1977, Susan Folstein and Michael Rutter conducted a study. In this study, they concluded that autism was prevalent in identical twins. In other words, they could figure that if one identical twin had autism, it was likely that both would; on the other hand, there was no occurrence of autism in both twins if they were non-identical. As a result of this study, Folstein and Rutter were able to evidence the importance of genetics when it comes to the development of autism. This is the most significant evidence to counter Kanner's parenting theory mentioned in 1967.

- In 1980, autism was entered into the Diagnostic and Statistical Manual (DSM) as a disorder separate from schizophrenia. This inclusion also indicated that not only was autism a particular developmental disorder but that hallucinations were not a common symptom associated with ASD. Furthermore, this development within the DSM categorized autism into four groups: childhood-onset pervasive developmental disorder, residual autism, infantile autism, and an atypical type.

- Seven years later, in 1987, the DSM-III was edited to broaden the scope of autism, adding a slew of minor symptoms into the mix. In this same year, Ivar Lovaas published a study indicating that symptoms of autism improved in children after undergoing intensive behavioral therapy. This modeled that autism could be "treated" in a sense, allowing children with the disorder to acclimate to the world more robustly than ever before.
- In 1988, the movie *Rain Man* came out. It surrounded the story of an autistic person with savant syndrome, which was a bit of a double-edged sword. While it did increase public awareness about autism, the movie also served to create stereotypes about autism.
- In 1990, Congress decreed that autism should be included as an educational disability. This is the year autism was recognized as an educational disability, which helped those with autism qualify for much-needed accommodations to help them navigate academia.

- In 1994, the DSM-IV included Asperger's disorder as a category under the umbrella of ASD.
- In 1998, Andrew Wakefield and associated colleagues suggested that the measles, mumps, and rubella vaccine might have predisposed children to autism. Similarly, in 2001, thimerosal was discontinued in childhood vaccines due to a suspected link to autism. However, it has been determined that vaccines were not responsible for autism. However, the controversy continues, with many parents still choosing not to vaccinate their children.
- In 2009, the Centers for Disease Control and Prevention (CDC) declared that 1 out of every 59 children had autism.
- In 2013, the DSM-V was released and combined all forms of autism into just ASD to cut down on diagnostic inconsistencies.

As you can tell, ASD has a rather complicated and deep history. It is not a new disorder; it has over a century of research behind it.

ASPERGER'S SYNDROME

You might hear people on the spectrum refer to themselves by the label of Asperger's. Asperger's was once a disorder that could be diagnosed, but it has been taken out of the DSM in recent years. This means no one can be diagnosed with it any longer, and for good reason. Often thought to be synonymous with "high functioning" autism, both terms have a rather harrowing connotation that stems from a cruel history. And while many people still cling to their Asperger's diagnosis, you will soon understand why that is not a positive thing.

As mentioned in the previous autism timeline, Asperger was the name of a psychiatrist in Vienna during the 1940s. It is no coincidence that during the 1940s, we experienced one of the darkest periods in history: World War II and the Holocaust.

To start, Hans Asperger did not describe what we have come to know today as Asperger's syndrome; instead, his work was recycled in the early '80s by psychiatrist Lorna Wing, prompting its inclusion in the DSM and other documentation. However, before that, Asperger and his diagnostic disorder were nothing to be proud of nor celebrated, as is often the case with a disorder named after oneself.

But let's go back even further to the period in which Asperger resided. Asperger was hugely complicit in euthanasia and eugenics during the Nazi occupation of Vienna, playing a role in sending children to their deaths for being "too disabled" due to autism. Asperger directly decided to transfer over a dozen children to a killing center in Vienna because of this, publicly stating that particularly disabled children should be killed.

At its core, Asperger's research was inspired by Nazi ideology. During the Third Reich, children were held to the standard of participating enthusiastically in Nazi ideology and propaganda. Psychiatrists employed by Nazis determined that some children, devoid of emotion or social feeling, could not join the community. Asperger thought classifying children this way was wrong at first, but later relented when he created the label of "autistic psychopathy" to describe the social detachment of these autistic children.

It is also notable that psychopathy was considered criminal in Nazi psychiatry, which makes sense when considering that Asperger thought autistic children to be sadistically evil. His diagnosis criteria did not stop there, only becoming harsher each year Nazism prevailed. He came as far as labeling "favorably autistic" children—which some consider "high functioning"—to be geniuses. At the same time, "unfavorable" or "low functioning" children were too defunct to let live. Furthermore, Asperger continued to promote the idea that autistic kids would never fit into the social community.

After the war, Wing found his research and named the disorder Asperger. To my dismay, it appears as though no one investigated the history of Hans Asperger before granting him a disorder bearing his name.

Therefore, the Asperger's label is defunct, and we are trying to move away from "high functioning" autism as a label as well. Both serve to identify nothing more than whether one would have survived the Nazi occupation; neither title is kind nor reliable to describe autism. Instead, people have adopted "high support needs" and "low support needs," reflecting the social shortcomings around the person rather than their abilities.

If someone you know proudly touts an Asperger's diagnosis, as many people do due to a perceived superiority behind it (many people consider Asperger's to be synonymous with "genius"), if you feel comfortable doing so, kindly inform them of the history behind that label. Furthermore, if a professional even attempts to diagnose your child with Asperger's, run as fast as you can; this is not a reputable practitioner nor a valid diagnosis post-2013.

ARE THERE MORE CASES OF AUTISM NOW?

Many people, especially older generations, refuse to accept an autism diagnosis of someone they know or are related to. This is because it seems to them that many more people are being diagnosed with the condition, which can prove problematic. If so many people are diagnosed with autism, how is it a valid disorder? This may be a concern you may have yourself, and it is a valid one to have. After all, no one explains *why* autism seems more prevalent.

The answer to "Are there more cases of autism now?" is not straightforward. It is a "yes and no" answer. On one hand, the diagnosis rate of autism has skyrocketed, and the Center for Disease Control and Prevention (CDC) confirms this; more cases of autism are being diagnosed than ever before (CDC, 2023a). But that does not mean there are more cases of autism than ever before. There are more diagnoses, but there aren't more cases.

The fact that we are experiencing an increase in diagnoses of autism is due predominantly to the fact that ASD is more commonly recognized now. In the past, parents did not know what to look for, nor did they suspect that autism could be the culprit behind their child behaving differently. The knowledge diffusion presented by the internet has allowed parents to become more intimately acquainted with myriad forms of information, opening the doors to more information than ever. This enables parents to look to autism as a potential explanation.

Some sources argue that birth conditions like weight and environmental factors can play a role in the perceived rise of autism cases. Overall, it is definite that while autism cases are not more plentiful, the diagnoses are—and that is a good thing! It means that more people than ever are getting help, and the world is becoming a safer and more nurturing place for people who experience differences in how their minds work. It is a good thing that the world is becoming more open to finding answers to questions parents like you have. Autism is nothing to be ashamed of!

Furthermore, there is more of a focus now on getting children treatment for ASD, which can explain why we see more diagnoses. Early treatment is crucial to help children acclimate to the world around them— a world that was unfortunately not built with them in mind. Naturally, parents and medical professionals will consider autism first. Luckily, ASD is not life-threatening and can empower parents to provide the help their children so desperately need.

No parent ever wishes to have an autistic child; it is not something we are prepared for. It is natural to fear the unknown, and most of us don't know much about autism; it's not something we learned in school. We also didn't learn to be parents before becoming parents; we learn as we go. Of course, as parents, we want to provide our children with everything we didn't have. We try to learn from our parents' mistakes so we can be even better parents than our parents were to us. We imagine our children's perfect life because we will provide them with love, education, and everything they need to succeed. However, as we already know, nothing is ever perfect! Even if your child is neurotypical, there is no such thing as an ideal life. I won't sugarcoat things; some challenges come with an ASD diagnosis. However, dealing with ASD does not have to be impossible; with the right tools and support system, you can help your child thrive.

This chapter provided some basic information about autism, including its history. Let's dive further into the symptoms and misconceptions surrounding ASD in the next chapter.

2

SYMPTOMS AND MISCONCEPTIONS OF AUTISM

As the parent of an autistic child—or as the parent of a child suspected to have autism—it can be hard to know what is and is not a symptom. Some days, it can seem like everything is a symptom of autism; on others, it can feel like your child is no different from any other child their age. Furthermore, misconceptions surrounding autism can confuse you—making it hard for you to know what your child needs. It also prevents others from understanding your struggles as a parent. The best way to be equipped to handle all of this is to understand how autism can present itself and the common misconceptions surrounding the disorder.

CHARACTERISTICS OF AUTISM

Identifying some of the critical signs of autism is essential to understanding the disorder. Whether you must identify signs to get a diagnosis for your child or if you are wondering whether a particular behavioral trait is a sign of your child's existing diagnosis, understanding the symptoms will allow you to understand the disorder in-depth. Let's talk about some of the predominant characteristics that someone with ASD may experience.

In children, many behavioral traits can indicate autism. Generally, these behaviors will seem restricted or repetitive in some capacity, and often, they seem unusual when observed (CDC, 2023b). For example, children with autism usually line up their toys in rows, even getting upset if their row or order is disturbed. This is a common habit for autistic children during playtime. This might not seem like playing to you, but to them, it is. Autistic children also tend to play with the same toys in the same way every time they pick them up. This is because they have deemed that that toy is for that specific purpose, and it makes perfect sense to them.

Another characteristic an autistic child may display is something called "echolalia." Echolalia occurs when a child becomes fixated on a word or phrase, repeating it over and over. This form of verbal stimming can help them feel comfortable; they may feel compelled to repeat this word or phrase consistently. Other forms of stimming include hand flapping, rocking back and forth, and spinning in circles.

Obsessive interest can also be attributed to autism; the child may be drawn to a specific toy or even part of a toy, wanting to only focus on or play with that particular item. When their routine or interest is altered, a child with autism can become very upset. Children with ASD may react unusually to specific sensory inputs—including textures, bright lights, foods, sounds, and scents.

There are also specific social and communication traits that children with autism often exhibit. For example, you might notice that your child struggles with making or maintaining eye contact. This is one of the most common social traits that an autistic child will have. You might also notice delayed social development. For example, they might not respond to their name or show facial expressions in early childhood. They may struggle with interactive games, hand gestures, or playing pretend. Something to look out for is a lack of empathy; if your child does not notice that other people are upset or hurt, that can also be a sign that indicates autism.

Overall, the social signs of autism are hard to distinguish, as they can often look like your child is just reserved—or they can even be symptoms of other disorders. This also makes it hard to diagnose autism based on social traits alone. When observing your child for social characteristics that can indicate autism, you will want to look for ones that primarily involve avoidance or a lack of observation.

Other traits that can indicate autism include:

- Language skills that are slower to develop than expected
- Movement skills that are slower to develop than expected
- Cognitive or learning skills that are slower to develop than expected
- Behavior characterized by hyperactivity, impulsiveness, and inattention
- Presence of epilepsy or a disorder characterized by seizures
- Unusual patterns of eating and sleeping
- Gastrointestinal problems such as constipation
- Unusual reactions or emotions

- Experiencing anxiety, stress, or excessive worry
- Either a lack of fear or heightened fear responses compared to what is typically expected

If you suspect that your child may have autism, one of the best things to do is to record their symptoms. This way, you will have something tangible to show a medical professional when you take them in for observation.

SIGNS TO LOOK FOR IN BABIES

Autism can be present in babies; there are notable signs you can look out for early on. By looking for early signs, you can speed up the process of receiving a diagnosis. This will make obtaining the resources your child needs easier as they advance through life. The signs of autism in babies and younger children can be distinguished easily by age group.

For example, there are numerous signs of autism in babies that you can look for between the ages of 6 and 12 months. You are going to want to look out for symptoms such as:

- **Unnatural or repetitive movements**: Your baby may begin with repetitive behaviors early, such as hand and foot movements that are atypical for an infant. If you notice your baby engaging in these repetitive movements, try writing down when and if they are correlated to anything else. For instance, some repetitive behaviors may be a method of coping with external stimuli.

- **Aversion to touch**: Aversion to touch is a common symptom of autism, as physical contact can be somewhat uncomfortable for those with the disorder. If your baby has an aversion to touch or cuddling with you, that may be an early indication of autism. Another sign that indicates a potential aversion to touch is that your baby will not reach up when you are about to pick them up, as this is the age at which that connection is formed.

- **Refusal to imitate actions**: Babies tend to imitate other people—it is the fastest way to learn and comes naturally to them. However, a baby who potentially has autism may not imitate you when you smile, laugh, play peek-a-boo, or anything similar.

- **Limited gesturing**: Babies often point at something they want, indicating that you should hand it to them. They'll also wave hello or goodbye to people in their lives, especially those close to them. However, in an infant with autism, these gestures will be limited; they may not wave or point, seeming disinterested in the things around them.

- **Limited verbal communication**: A neurotypical baby will try to imitate the sounds of people talking, even if they cannot say their first words. A baby with autism will not be very verbal; they may not chatter or imitate sounds, but it might seem that your child is quiet at first sight. In some rare instances, babies with autism don't cry often, although not common; if this happens with your child, let their doctor know immediately.

- **Overreacting to noise**: It is not rare for someone with autism to be averse to loud sounds. If a sound that would not usually bother a baby elicits crying or other adverse reactions in your infant child, this may be another indication of autism.

- **Not responding to their name**: By 6-12 months old, a baby should respond to their name somehow, whether by turning their head or indicating that they heard you. A baby with autism might not do this, either because they do not realize that it is their name or because they do not realize that you expect a reaction from them.

As your child ages, there will be more signs as they approach the later stages of their infancy and the early stages of toddlerhood. Some things to keep an eye out for in children up to 2 years include:

- **Limited or absent speech**: By this age, your child should be speaking in some capacity. If they rarely use verbal communication or do not/cannot communicate verbally at all, that is a significant sign that your child may have autism.
- **Walking on their toes**: Many people with autism walk on their toes rather than using the whole foot.
- **Difficulty following instructions**: By this age, your child should be able to follow and carry out simple verbal instructions such as "throw it away," "get your shoes," etc. If they struggle with the ability to do so for whatever reason, this can be a clear sign of autism.
- **An intense focus on one object or subject to the exclusion of all else**: It is not uncommon

for people with autism to hyper-focus on one or two things at a time. This is referred to as a special interest.

Other signs may indicate autism, but these are the most common and easiest to notice. However, don't look at this list as your only resource because each child is different, and your child's characteristics may not be as prominent. One thing I didn't know then that I know now is that if your child does not show noticeable symptoms, you may have to look deeper. For example, my daughter made eye contact, but as you continued speaking to her, she would lose interest and focus on something else; I did not know this was also a sign of autism. I thought that if she made eye contact, everything was OK. She also pointed at things, but not consistently; sometimes she would, sometimes she wouldn't, and eventually she stopped altogether. I thought things were OK if she was pointing in any capacity. No one ever explained to me that these things must be done consistently; if your child does these things intermittently, bring up these concerns to their doctor. If you don't like the doctor's response, look for a second opinion. If anything in your gut makes you uneasy about your child's behavior, bring it to their doctor and start documenting it. This can help open the doors to an evaluation and allow the doctor to determine if something else is happening.

EVERYONE IS DIFFERENT

As you think about the signs and symptoms of autism, there is something essential to remember: not everyone with autism will have the same symptoms, nor will they experience them in the same way. Two autistic children —much like two autistic adults—are bound to have very different experiences from one another. This is because, as mentioned earlier, autism is a spectrum disorder. As I discussed before, I, too, have fallen victim to the comparisons; don't do it! Making comparisons is natural; our mind tricks us when we fear the unknown. We always try to return to something we know because it gives us a sense of reassurance, but every child is different, and a child with autism will be very different from another child with autism. Treat them as the individuals that they are.

The reason that I tell you this is two-fold. First, acknowledging that everyone is different will help you get your child the proper treatment for them. Having expectations that your child "should" act a certain way is only going to hold them back; instead, focus on how they behave. Second, treating people with autism as if they should fit a mold hurts the autism community.

Many people with autism already feel out of place for being neurodivergent, and by acknowledging that everyone is different, you can help your child understand that there is nothing wrong with them being autistic—they are just different, making them beautiful and unique!

It is also good to remember that not all children displaying some autism characteristics have autism. I know children who have had a speech delay and did not have autism. I also know children who walk on their tiptoes and are not autistic, and the list goes on and on. The point is that having one or a couple of autistic characteristics does not mean a child is autistic. It is crucial to observe the behaviors, and if they continue to display characteristics of autism and, in addition, start to develop other autistic traits, there should be a valid concern. While I want you to be informed, I don't want you to jump to conclusions because your child does one little thing that could signal autism.

AUTISM MISCONCEPTIONS

As unfortunate as it is, there are numerous misconceptions surrounding ASD. Breaking down these misconceptions is crucial for you to understand as a parent. Even if you don't believe these misconceptions, understanding why they are incorrect empowers you to educate others. Let's look at some of the most common misconceptions surrounding autism and why they are wrong.

Misconception 1: Autism Is a Childhood Disorder

Many people believe that autism can only be diagnosed in children, even thinking it magically disappears as someone ages. This is entirely untrue; not only are more adults being diagnosed with autism due to our improved understanding of the condition, but there is no reason that autism would go away with age. Additionally, many children are wrongly diagnosed with conditions like attention deficit/hyperactivity disorder or social anxiety, only to have their diagnosis updated to ASD when they get older. This is because, as I mentioned, it is rather complicated to diagnose autism; there is no specific test for it because an ASD diagnosis is arrived at by observing behaviors. Furthermore, some researchers indicate that autism can seemingly become more severe with age (or more pronounced) due to circumstances in life.

Thinking that ASD is a disorder that exists only in childhood is entirely erroneous. It is plausible to be diagnosed well into adulthood for many reasons—some people believe an adult ASD diagnosis is invalid, but this is not true. It is also possible that a child diagnosed with autism can improve some or most of the characteristics of autism; this can be due to the help they receive through therapy and the child's development. Some children might even get to a point where they don't display enough ASD characteristics to be considered autistic. This does not mean the child outgrew the disorder; it just means that the characteristics of autism are not as pronounced as they once were, and the child no longer needs additional support to navigate life. While this does happen, it's not the norm. As parents, we shouldn't think about the day our child will miraculously show no signs of autism; this might not be the case for our child. It is essential to understand our child as an individual and not compare them to any other child, whether the other child is neurotypical or neurodiverse.

Misconception 2: Is It Something in the Air?

Another common misconception surrounding autism is that something in the air or environment—like the water we drink—is causing autism in children. This leads to another misconception that more kids are "getting" autism—even though it is not a condition that you can "get" or "catch." The truth is that more children are being diagnosed today than ever before, but this has more to do with our budding medical knowledge of the condition than any environmental cause ever would. As

I mentioned in the previous chapter, we know more now and can better diagnose people of all ages with ASD.

Furthermore, no evidence suggests that the increased rate at which diagnoses occur has anything to do with environmental factors. Professionals state that we perceive an increase in these diagnoses because we have broadened the horizon of the disorder, including more and more symptoms to represent the condition accurately. Scientific evidence that air, water, or food-based sources are causing autism is lacking, clarifying that there isn't something in the air causing children to "catch" an autism bug.

Misconception 3: Vaccines Cause Autism

This has been one of the most controversial claims surrounding autism to date. I mentioned in the autism timeline in the last chapter that certain mercury-based ingredients in vaccines were thought to be linked to autism; however, that connection has been studied, and no objective evidence has been found to suggest that vaccines are linked to autism. However, many people still believe vaccines are linked to autism. I strongly believe in free choice; you must always do what is best for your child. I suggest basing your decisions on facts and research, not on what others say. Everyone reacts differently; people can be allergic or sensitive to something. This does not mean you will have the same experience. Therefore, we can't base our decisions on someone else's experience. On the other hand, you have every right to question anything and everything, and your decision should be yours to make after considering the facts and the pros and cons.

Misconception 4: Autism and Severe Intellectual Disabilities Are the Same

Many people believe that most people with ASD have severe intellectual disabilities. Despite the commonality of this misconception, it is not valid. Most people with autism can function "normally" and do not have significant intellectual disabilities. In some Eastern cultures, however, they only consider the most severe cases to be "true autism," therefore, these cultures think autistic people have an intellectual disability. This distinction is why many people wrongfully believe all autistic people have intellectual disabilities.

A similar misconception flows in the other direction —many people believe those with autism are savants or highly gifted, even possessing photographic or eidetic memories accompanying their autism. This is also a misconception, as this impacts such a small portion of the autistic community. By believing that all autistic people are highly gifted, much like thinking that all autistic people have an intellectual disability, one can perpetuate a harmful stereotype. The best way to fight this misconception is by understanding that all people with autism are individuals, and no one thing applies to everyone across the board.

Misconception 5: Everyone Experiences ASD the Same

The idea that everyone who has ASD has the same experiences is another wrong misconception. The reality is that everyone with autism experiences it differently—from the symptoms to the struggles they face in their daily lives. Autism causes differences within the brain, and no two brains are the same, just like no two cases of autism are the same. No one with autism can speak about what it is like for everyone—they can only talk about their own experiences.

This is another reason why it is so crucial to treat people as the individuals they are rather than their diagnosis.

These are not all the misconceptions surrounding ASD, but they are the most common ones. Remember that it is always important to research before you believe what someone tells you about a condition—especially if they are not medical professionals. If you encounter someone who seems to think in one of these misconceptions, it is up to you to educate them. I recommend doing so kindly and with an open heart, as this will make them more receptive to learning.

Overall, the misconceptions surrounding autism are not beneficial to the autism community or society as a whole—they make it harder to understand what the condition entails and place unfair expectations on people with the disorder. Breaking down these misconceptions can make the world more understanding and open for neurodiverse individuals.

CAUSES OF AUTISM

There's a lot of contention surrounding the causes of autism. Many blame vaccines and medicine, while others blame lousy parenting and environmental factors. It is essential to understand that there is no single cause for autism. Not everyone with autism has autism due to the same reasons or characteristics.

One of the main risk factors associated with autism is genetics. Autism seemingly runs in families, which means that if your child has autism, it is likely that you or their other parent does, or you may carry a gene change that can be responsible for the development of autism regardless of whether you have the disorder. Sometimes, though, autism can arise spontaneously during the conception and development of your child in utero. However, it is essential to note that these gene changes are not typically the sole cause of autism; they usually increase a child's risk of developing autism.

Environmental risk factors can also be responsible for the development of autism, but these are not the sole cause on their own, either. Genetic predisposition can make environmental factors more likely to correlate with the development of autism. In general, one of the following must be present to increase the chances that a child will develop autism significantly:

- **Advanced age in either parent**: Parents older than the norm at conception are more likely to produce autistic offspring.
- **Pregnancy complications**: Anything from prematurity, low birth weight, and multiple births such as twins or triplets.
- **Pregnancies close together**: Pregnancies that occur within a year of one another increase the likelihood that the younger child will develop autism.

It is essential to know that no matter the cause, autism is not your "fault"—it is no one's fault, and there is nothing wrong with having an autistic child. One of the most essential pieces of advice I can give you is never feeling bad about your child's condition. Your child will thrive—it will take a lot of patience, tenacity, and openness to build structure and routine on your part. In addition, you must adapt to the needs of your child and your family. As mentioned before, not all children will experience autism the same way, and the requirements of one individual will differ from those of another on the spectrum. As you understand your child's behavior, you will start to identify what triggers certain behaviors. You will realize that your child is not bratty, and they are not having tantrums; they are having a meltdown caused by sensory overload, frustration because they cannot communicate their needs or wants, or anything else that causes them to feel overwhelmed. As you understand your child's triggers, you will understand how to calm them down after a meltdown or how to avoid the triggers altogether. There isn't a one-size-fits-all when parenting an autistic child. It is best to have a lot of patience, learn to understand your child and their behaviors, and you should learn to identify their primary triggers. Knowing what helps them feel regulated will also be extremely helpful. This will look different for every child, but you can do further research to find regulating toys and items such as a swing, cushions, weighted blankets, rocking chair, yoga ball, sensory mats, fidgeting toys, etc., that will work for your child. There are many items for this purpose; some things will work for your child, some will not, and it is up to you to figure out what items will be most suitable for your child.

Misconceptions Surrounding the Causes of Autism

Just as there are misconceptions about autism, there are many misconceptions that surround the causes of autism. Many people wrongfully believe certain things contribute to the likelihood of developing autism when they don't!

One major misconception surrounding the causes of autism is that it is caused by bad parenting or something called "refrigerator mothers": mothers who are emotionally distant or cold. The idea behind this misconception is that if your child has autism, there must be something wrong with you or how you parent. This is such a horrible misconception, and it is also such an outdated way to think. The assumption from the autism timeline that parenting causes autism has been debunked repeatedly, proving that parenting has nothing to do with autism or the likelihood that your child will develop it. Even the best parents in the world can have autistic children; it is in no way a reflection of you or your parenting skills.

There is another misconception that environmental factors solely cause autism; this is also untrue. Genes and family lineage are more likely to indicate a child's likelihood of being autistic. You can rest easy knowing that the city you live in will not cause your child to be autistic.

It is essential to understand that it is not just the signs and symptoms you must watch out for but the misconceptions surrounding autism as well. As the parent of an autistic child, many people will misunderstand your child, accidentally or intentionally. It is your job as a parent to guide your child through these scenarios, letting them know that sometimes people can be unintentionally mean because of their ignorance, and things they believe or say are untrue about ASD. It is also essential to enlighten your child with the truth about their diagnosis. Your child needs to understand that they are different from neurotypical children, but there is nothing wrong with that, and all it means is that they process things differently. This must be done at the right age. A small child is not likely to understand this, but explaining things to them as they age is essential. I wish all parents would be conscious or cared enough to teach all children about differences. Just as a neurodiverse child should understand that they interpret things differently, a neurotypical child should know that a neurodiverse child interprets things differently. This would prevent neurotypical kids from treating neurodiverse kids as "weird" and excluding them from play and other activities.

With this knowledge, you are far more equipped to tackle the road ahead of you regarding your child and their autism. Now that you understand both the signs and significant misconceptions surrounding autism, it is essential to dive into the gender gap and why men are seemingly more prone to it than women.

3

THERE ARE MORE AUTISTIC MALES THAN FEMALES—FACT OR FICTION?

Many firmly believe that men are more likely to have autism than women, that autism is a male-dominated disorder, and that it is rare for a woman to have autism. As it turns out, these beliefs are only valid if you squint—an issue that runs far more profound than it seems. Rather than autism being rare in women, it falls to the case of girls being misdiagnosed due to a long history of dismissing and misdiagnosing females. It is important to note that girls show different symptoms and are often better at masking, which makes it rather difficult for professionals to diagnose ASD in females. Let's talk about what is going on and why it can seem like autism is more male-dominated when that is not the case.

A LONG, HARD HISTORY

One of the biggest reasons people believe that women are less likely to have autism is due to the historical precedent surrounding the condition. Studies about autism have always focused on male experiences, and there are many reasons for this. One of those reasons is that women were viewed as too fragile to be test subjects—even in infancy—which has resulted in a stunning lack of scientific evidence and research surrounding the idiosyncratic experiences of women. Medicine has had a long, complex history of dismissing and misdiagnosing symptoms in females, which stems from the fact that treatment has always been male-dominated—a result of sexist societal structures that kept women from accessing academia and medicine alike.

It is also interesting to note the deep history of "female hysteria" in medicine. And by interesting, I mean disturbing because the prevalent hysteria diagnoses that dominated female medicine for decades did far more harm than good. Essentially, a woman would be diagnosed with hysteria for any emotional, hormonal, sexual, or any symptoms that did not indicate an apparent condition; this promoted the idea that women are "crazy" and overly emotional.

Even today, we can see similar mistreatment in medicine regarding females. Rather than taking the time to listen to concerns, it is not uncommon for a male doctor to place a woman's problems in the hands of it being "just her hormones" or "normal," when, in fact, a woman can be suffering from severe pain or a serious health condition. This is even more prevalent in women of color.

As a result, modern studies tend to focus on the male experience rather than the female experience. We're still working on updating scientific bodies of knowledge regarding more "common" or "well-known" issues like anxiety and depression; it will take even longer for our body of knowledge to update its data surrounding autism. This is not intended to invalidate the male experience with autism by placing it on a back burner; instead, it is necessary to fight for appropriate recognition of women's equal struggles with autism and their overall health. It is worth mentioning that autism is not the only condition in which females demonstrate different symptoms than males. This is also the case with heart attacks, multiple sclerosis, stroke, and pain, to name a few.

WOMEN EXPERIENCE DIFFERENT SYMPTOMS

Besides medical neglect and historical issues within the medical system, there is another reason women are not being diagnosed with autism as much as men are—and it has nothing to do with autism being a rare condition for women. One of the biggest reasons women are fundamentally misdiagnosed or underdiagnosed when it comes to autism is the fact that not only do women display different symptoms than men, but women are often better at masking. Women are naturally more social than men. Let's examine the most prominent reasons that make it seem more males have autism than females.

Why should anyone know that women and men are *different* regarding disorders and other health factors? A primary reason more women fail to receive ASD diagnoses than men is their intelligence quotient (IQ). In boys, signs of autism more frequently appear as outward symptoms like behavioral issues or struggles. For girls, however, the battle is more internal. The girls diagnosed usually display signs more closely to how boys experience autism. Namely, developmental delays and behavioral issues will get a girl diagnosed quickly. On the other hand, females with higher IQs are left on the sidelines.

This is because, for women and girls with autism and a higher IQ, behavioral issues rarely show. Therefore, these individuals do not stand out as much, meaning they are less likely to receive a diagnosis. Instead, females with autism and a high IQ will observe their surroundings, making assessments that help them cope with daily life and learning to imitate others to ease social expectations. For instance, a lot of autistic women become masters at small talk. This can make it much easier to navigate the expectations society has placed on them. Furthermore, females with autism are likely to tolerate situations that make them uncomfortable more often than males are, putting in more effort to seem "normal," which makes it hard for women to receive a diagnosis at any stage in life.

This brings me to another prominent reason females are less likely to be diagnosed with autism: they display more "socially acceptable" behaviors despite their disorder. Many women with ASD are prone to engaging in activities alone, making them seem timid and docile and keeping them out of the public eye. Reading, academia, and homemaking behaviors are all common hobbies of autistic females, which can seem relatively "normal" in the eyes of a society that still emphasizes gender roles. While there is an expectation that males should be outgoing, there is also an expectation that females should be introverted, which means that many of the default behaviors of autistic women are over-looked and seen as typical.

Additionally, it may be the case that females show less repetitive or restricted behaviors than males. When an autistic little girl plays with her toys, it can look quite normal because, at first glance, it looks like she's just organizing or playing as anyone else would. But if you put her next to a girl who is not on the spectrum, you will notice they have contrasting play manners. This subtle difference means that autism in females is frequently swept under the rug. When boys with autism play, their behaviors are far more noticeable.

Out of all the explanations for the disparity between males and females in getting an ASD diagnosis, perhaps the most impactful cause is that women are often better than men at masking. Masking is a common tactic used by people with ASD. It involves suppressing behaviors that are soothing or otherwise characteristic of ASD to make oneself seem more "normal" or acceptable to society. Women are better at this than men—at least generally speaking—because females are societally shaped to be more social. As I mentioned, women with higher IQs are better at navigating social situations, allowing their ASD symptoms to fly under the radar.

Overall, there are a lot of factors that contribute to the fact that women are diagnosed less than men. However, that does not mean that more men have autism.

Modern experts are not purposely neglecting females and their experiences. They do not have the textbook knowledge needed to address the female experience with autism, leading many women to be misdiagnosed with other conditions such as depression and anxiety—which are mere symptoms of their autism.

In my daughter's case, we brought up autism concerns to her pediatrician after 12 months because we noticed she started stimming by flapping her hands and rocking her body back and forth. Now, this alone would not prove that she was autistic, but we did bring up the concern to her pediatrician. My niece used to flap her hands and rock her body, but she stopped doing it at three. At the time, although I was a little concerned about my daughter's stimming, it wasn't a primary concern because I thought that, like my niece, she would probably outgrow it. When the concerns were brought up to her pediatrician, he dismissed them, stating that she made eye contact when you spoke to her, responded to her name, said her first word at nine months, walked by the time she was 12 months, etc. He emphasized all the milestones that made her "normal" but did not look deeper into other things that could potentially exhibit signs of autism. This was comforting to hear as a parent, and we continued to believe our daughter was not autistic—partly because we wanted to believe she was not autistic in our hearts and partly because we didn't know enough about autism to prove the pediatrician wrong.

I also want to point out that her pediatrician was not the only professional who missed the ASD diagnosis for our daughter. Once her pediatrician realized that the stimming was not improving and saw a "pattern" to her stimming, he became concerned that she might have seizures, so he referred us to a neurologist. We saw three doctors in the same office because no one could figure out what was wrong with our daughter, and they consulted with one another. She had an electroencephalogram (EEG) scan of her brain, which returned normal. The doctors didn't know what to make of it, and rather than focusing on her behavior, they wanted to run more tests. I opposed more testing because I knew more testing would not give us the answer we sought. Additionally, she would have to be sedated entirely due to her young age, which is very dangerous for a 2-year-old. They had already asked us to try CBD oil and cough syrup to help with the repeated motions. Seeing that they were guessing, the next course of action they recommended did not settle well with me. Although my husband and I disagreed on the path of action at the beginning, we were on the same page once he understood how invasive the test was and how dangerous it is for a young child to be fully sedated. I am not saying that a child should not undergo this kind of testing if they need it; sometimes, these tests can be lifesaving. This wasn't the case for our daughter, and I knew we would still not get the answers we sought.

Due to us refusing additional testing, we were finally referred to the Regional Center in California. The Regional Center provided assessments from Speech Pathologists, Occupational Therapists, and Behavioral Psychologists. It wasn't until then that an ASD diagnosis was reached. The difference between the testing done by her doctor and the neurologists as opposed to the testing from the professionals provided by the Regional Center is that the pediatrician and the neurologists focused on what our daughter was doing and not what she wasn't. The pediatrician and neurologist also considered her stimming a tick or a sign of seizures. They went down the textbook list of common ASD characteristics, and because she didn't show the prominent symptoms, they didn't dig deeper. Every child will experience autism differently. I cannot stress this enough!

I do not intend to attack healthcare professionals; I believe it is not their fault they were given few tools to recognize autism properly. As stated before, most of the characteristics doctors and other healthcare professionals look for are based on studies mainly from a male perspective. They are also given a handful of factors to base their opinion on. Most professionals are unaware that they should look for different characteristics in females. I also want to emphasize that my daughter's story is not the only one with this outcome. My goddaughter's diagnosis was also missed by her pediatrician; in her case, her pediatrician was female. Her pediatrician was insistent that she was not autistic, and when she finally learned of my goddaughter's diagnosis, she felt awful. I have also heard from other parents at my daughter's school that they faced similar situations; this applied to girls and boys. If the child does not display the "basic" symptoms of autism, healthcare professionals are not equipped with the knowledge to dig deeper. You can be sure that doctors and healthcare professionals are not purposely misdiagnosing children. We need to create more awareness of this problem so that the educating bodies and researchers can address it.

MENTAL HEALTH IMPACTS

Imagine having to pretend to be someone or something you are not. Fundamentally, you know that the way you are acting is not you, and you would love to be in touch and connected to who you are. But on the outside, you *must* pretend and act like someone else—because society does not understand why you behave the way you do, and they might call you weird or believe you to be dangerous. Imagine having to keep these emotions crammed inside, with no one to trust or talk to about it, silently trapped within the prison of yourself while playing pretend with everyone around you. Wouldn't that be terrible?

Unfortunately, this is the reality many autistic women deal with, often from birth. Dealing with undiagnosed autism, or even unrecognized autism, can be very upsetting, causing myriad mental health issues. Many females are first diagnosed with anxiety or depression —often treatment-resistant anxiety or depression—far before they are considered autistic. This happens because, due to their undiagnosed autism, many women develop depression and anxiety. In some cases, however, symptoms of autism are dismissed as depression or anxiety; this can be the case when they display isolating tendencies.

Living with any disorder, illness, or condition can be debilitating, but the impacts of undiagnosed autism on mental health can be much worse. Years of one's life can be wasted on feeling like something is wrong with you or that you are a mess. Only to find out later that there is nothing "wrong" with you—you are just autistic, and that is okay! However, not having access to the resources, help, and information surrounding ASD can make it very hard to live with the disorder. Because of this, it is essential to spread awareness about the disparities between women and autism diagnoses; it can help prevent women from going their entire lifetimes without the proper help. You are taking an excellent first step in ensuring your child has an adequate diagnosis for their needs.

The good news is that further research is constantly being conducted. Fortunately, the enigma of autism and females is starting to be addressed. Every day, we get closer to reaching equality when diagnosing women.

This chapter taught you about the long, problematic history surrounding women and autism. Generally, it is a misconception that autism is more prevalent in males; men are just diagnosed at a higher rate due to the research and studies primarily revolving around them. Now you know how and why this misconception exists. In the next chapter, we will explore another community that lacks equality in receiving an ASD diagnosis: marginalized groups and people of color.

The Gift You Can Give Other Parents

"Autism is as much a part of humanity as is the capacity to dream."

— *KATHLEEN SEIDEL*

Cast your mind back to when your child was first diagnosed with autism. How did you feel?

When my daughter was diagnosed, I felt lost. I knew a little about autism, but I had no idea how to support my little girl. I wanted her to thrive, but I was clueless about how to help her.

I think this is the most scary thing about receiving an autism diagnosis for your child. You have this overwhelming urge to help them, but you have no idea how. When I realized that not only could I handle the challenge, but I could help other parents too, I learned that I was far stronger and more capable than I realized.

You're going to find that too, and I'd like to ask you to help me give that gift to more parents.

There are so many parents out there feeling exactly like you and I did when our children were first diagnosed.

They're looking for this guidance, and we can help them to find it easily.

By leaving a review of this book on Amazon, you'll show other parents where they can find all the information they need to put their minds at ease and help their children thrive.

People are searching for the books that will help them, and it's reviews like yours that make those books visible – so your help is going to go a long way.

Thank you so much for your support. Parenting is always going to have its challenges, but together, we can make sure an autism diagnosis isn't one of them.

Scan the QR code here

4

DISPARITIES IN DIAGNOSIS AND TREATMENT IN MARGINALIZED COMMUNITIES AND PEOPLE OF COLOR

Women are not the only community that faces striking disparity when it comes to the diagnosis of autism. Marginalized communities (including people of color) face difficulties getting adequate care for ASD. The lack of access to healthcare, stigma, and other socioeconomic barriers primarily contribute to a lack of or delayed evaluation and services for ASD.

RACIAL DIFFERENCES IN ASD

When you first glance at statistics, they indicate that more white people have autism than any other race. However, it is essential to remember that statistics can be skewed in many ways, and this seems to be the case with statistics indicating racial differences in autism.

While it may seem like autism is more prevalent in white people, this statistic is due to various sampling errors. Much like the case with women, it is also the case that marginalized communities are not recognized as actively for ASD symptoms.

According to various sources, autism is 1.1 times more likely to be diagnosed in white children than in black children and 1.2 times more likely in white children than in Hispanic children (CDC, 2018). These statistics illustrate that white people are more likely "to be diagnosed" rather than more likely for autism "to occur" in them. This is due to the diagnosis rates not accurately reflecting the actual prevalence of the disorder. Simultaneous studies prove that stigma and lack of access to healthcare services caused by low income, citizenship limitations, and language barriers contribute significantly to why children of color, especially Hispanic children—experience difficulties receiving proper treatment.

The difference in how ASD is regarded among white children and children of color is dramatic and leads to autistic children not getting the services and help they need. Black and Hispanic children are continuously diagnosed less than white children, which is the prime indication that there is some fundamental barrier to a lack of medical treatment. Furthermore, it is essential to consider racial stereotypes' role in making it difficult for children of color to receive diagnoses. In white children, autistic behaviors may be identified more readily, whereas children of color may have the same traits perceived as violent. This long-standing concept results from harmful racial stereotypes in medicine and psychiatry.

However, there is some good news regarding the disparities between races in ASD diagnoses. Around 2006, the prevalence ratio—the number that indicates the likelihood of a condition between two different groups–was at an all-time high. This means that there was a significantly higher rate of difference in diagnosis for black and white children and an even higher rate of difference between white and Hispanic children. However, as the years have passed, that gap has slowly closed, and today, it is about 1.1 and 1.2 times, respectively, as mentioned earlier (CDC, 2018).

This means that research and studies have increased, bringing us closer to a state of equality between the races—closely resembling the closing gap between men and women with ASD. More and more children, regardless of barriers, are getting the help they need. However, these barriers should not be disregarded, as the battle is not over.

The most significant and most prominent explanation for why children of color are diagnosed at a lower rate than white children is socioeconomic barriers such as finances, citizenship, language, etc. Because of these differences, autism can take a back burner in a family's life and go unnoticed by professionals. After all, you can't get a diagnosis if you never have the chance to see a doctor.

A CLOSER LOOK

Let's take a closer look at some of the reasons that children of color are diagnosed at a lower rate than white children.

Income plays a significant role when it comes to children belonging to a minority group receiving a diagnosis. Lower-income families face various circumstances that make seeking medical attention rather tricky. For example, medical visits are often costly, even with insurance. This can mean that a family may not have the money to afford a medical visit over something easily dismissed as a behavioral issue. In addition, lower-income families require all adults in the household to have a full-time job—in this case, who has time to take the child to the doctor for a non-urgent issue?

Beyond that, low-income families often have seemingly more significant issues than a child who can potentially have autism. Between trying to make ends meet, ensuring the children stay in school, and more, autism does not seem to be the first thing on a parent's mind. They're more worried about keeping food on the table, and who can blame them? This speaks significantly to the systematic failings that prevent low-income people from affording potentially life-altering medical attention. And this is only one piece of the complex puzzle that explains why minority children are often left behind in ASD diagnoses.

Another primary reason children of color are less likely to receive a diagnosis is limited access to information. The information surrounding autism and its signs—especially idiosyncrasies that exist along the spectrum—is already slim. Even well-off, affluent families struggle to access this information; communities with less access to medical care, the Internet, etc., will struggle even more. This limited access to information makes it hard for parents and children. Parents don't know that the signs their child exhibits indicate something may be amiss.

Furthermore, historical practices in low-income communities have led to limited access to resources and quality health care in marginalized neighborhoods.

Due to redistricting, government funding issues, etc., marginalized communities have always had less access to medical resources. It's hard enough for people of color to receive primary medical care; getting access to more "niche" medical care, like an ASD diagnosis, will only be more challenging.

Discrimination is another factor in the inability of children from marginalized communities to receive a diagnosis. Unfortunately, discrimination is not uncommon in medical circles, which means it can be challenging for children to receive a diagnosis if they are not white, regardless of any other circumstances. As I mentioned earlier, autism symptoms may be dismissed as "racially appropriate" behaviors, which is quite disgraceful today.

The fear of stigma and uncertainty regarding the diagnostic process rounds out the struggles of marginalized communities in connection to ASD diagnoses. Marginalized communities are sidelined; stereotypes and discrimination are unfair yet prevalent within society and are still a reality in marginalized communities. Parents might also worry about getting their child diagnosed due to stigma and uncertainty about the process holistically, which causes additional problems.

Sometimes, parents may purposely avoid medical help for their child's condition, even if the signs of autism are more pronounced. For example, many parents fear that if a child is diagnosed, they will be treated differently by social exclusion from peers and within the school system. Moreover, the stigma and stereotypes surrounding ASD and marginalized communities can contribute to attributing behavioral issues to the child being "bratty" or "moody," dismissing any medical concerns. Some parents think that a child will outgrow their symptoms, while others allow themselves to be influenced by family members to believe that their child is just spoiled or acting out. The fear and stigma surrounding the diagnostic process contribute very heavily to the inability of children to receive the help they need.

To sum it up, financial issues, discrimination, and the fear of stigma and uncertainty contribute massively to the disparities in diagnosis that people of color face.

OTHER DIAGNOSTIC DELAYS

These factors are not the only culprits for diagnostic delays, either. Other pressing factors impede a diagnosis; some apply systemically, while others predominantly affect marginalized groups. The American Association of Pediatrics recommends a universal developmental ASD screening be implemented. According to this implementation, all children would undergo an autism screening at a certain age, and their pediatrician would continue to monitor their development after that. In theory, this sounds like a great idea, as it would ensure that all children have equal access to ASD screening. However, in practice, it doesn't quite work out that way.

First, cost continues to play a role in preventing certain groups from getting the healthcare they need. Insurance is not accessible in most cases either; there are virtually no options for a family with no spare money for a doctor's visit. Second, as professionals continue to lack confidence in identifying symptoms, it will be difficult for kids to get the help they need. Suppose parents are unsure about what to look for, and they look to professionals for guidance, and the professionals are not confident about symptoms that are not obvious. In that case, it can be a lengthy and stressful process. This is one of the reasons that I am writing this book; the only way to overcome this barrier is to spread awareness. The third obstacle is the lack of familiarity with screening tools. Parents are unaware of the tools available to get a diagnosis, and even having a diagnosis can be problematic because parents feel lost with no guidance.

Another reason diagnostic delays are further perpetuated is the "wait-and-see" approach. This approach encourages parents to wait for further symptoms before taking their child in for a diagnosis. This approach would theoretically work, allowing you to be sure before taking your child for screening. But in practice, this approach will only delay an already lengthy process. Early diagnosis has so much power, mainly because it allows you to get resources early, which can improve your child's life.

Many people, especially women and people of color, learn to mask much better as they age. If you wait to see more symptoms in your child before taking them in for a diagnosis, there may be nothing to see if your child has already learned to mask their behavior. Moreover, when you "see" symptoms, the damage may already be done; years of living with undiagnosed autism can cause severe trauma. It is best to steer clear of the "wait-and-see" approach as this will only delay your child from accessing the resources and the help they need. Even if your child does not have autism, they might have a speech delay, anxiety, or other conditions that should be addressed.

One of the main issues with early identification of autism is a lack of diversity in healthcare and its implicit bias. Lack of diversity contributes massively to marginalized communities' issues because so few doctors belong to these communities. Parents may not trust that white doctors can genuinely resonate with or identify the experiences of their child, and they are not wrong—many white doctors are so used to treating white males that they are not sure how to work with anyone else in an empathetic and understanding manner.

Implicit bias also contributes profoundly to the inability to get a proper diagnosis. Implicit bias refers to our subconscious bias, which includes stereotypes and attitudes that impact how we understand the world around us and our actions or decisions without being aware of them. Implicit bias can be favorable and unfavorable, although these biases tend to harm people of color. Common discrimination in medical care, for instance, assumes that those with bigger bodies have health issues solely about weight, thus refusing to hear any concerns they voice that do not revolve around weight issues. The same thing can happen when a family who is not white goes in for an autism screening, especially when the doctor is white.

A PREVALENT DISMISSAL OF CONCERN

In addition to what has been discussed thus far, there is another component to keep in mind. There are significant and terrible reports of the dismissal of concern by doctors when it comes to parents discussing their children's behavior (Aylward et al., 2021). Perhaps unsurprisingly, this dismissal impacts autism more than any other disability. Often, a parent will come to a doctor with concerns over their child's development or behavior, only to have it brushed off as usual or unnoteworthy. Unfortunately, a doctor can easily dismiss anything after observing your child for a few minutes, completely disregarding a parent's experience with their child's behavior. Sure, parents are not usually medical professionals, but who would know more about their child's behavior?

This experience, of course, does not include only children of color and other marginalized communities. Parents of all races, genders, and backgrounds have reported this striking medical negligence on the part of their doctor when it comes to ASD. And ASD is one of the only disorders with such a high margin of diagnosis error.

The most unfortunate aspect of this occurrence is that, as professionals, doctors can sow seeds of doubt within the parents' minds. What if they were wrong, and their child is just fine? How silly of them to think otherwise… right? Doctors have this power over us, which can cause many parents to avoid seeking a second opinion. Earlier, I discussed the experiences with my daughter, goddaughter, and other children at my daughter's school. Getting second, third, or even fourth opinions is crucial until you are confident that a doctor is correct —either because you have received a diagnosis or because they have provided you with a reasonable answer for your concerns without invalidating them.

RACIAL DIFFERENCES IN ASD CONSIDERATIONS

If all I have mentioned thus far is insufficient, specific racial differences exist when exploring how autism impacts children's ability to be diagnosed. The racial disparities in perceptions of autism can prove to be somewhat problematic; let's see why.

Studies about the perceptions of autism indicate that white parents are more open to the idea of their child being autistic than parents of other races (Autism Speaks, n.d.). In these studies, it was determined that while all parents who showed up were concerned with their child's level of communication, behavioral challenges, and more, white parents were more likely to concede that their children may have autism than black, Hispanic, Asian, or other racial groups of parents.

Additionally, it was noted that white children whose parents recognized the symptoms of autism early on experienced fewer struggles in life than children of parents who did not notice. In other words, children whose parents identified symptoms of autism early—as occurred most often in white families—tend to have fewer autism-related symptoms. On the other hand, children of color did not have positive outcomes even if their parents could identify autism early on. It is thought that the disparities in medical access, as described earlier, have been responsible for these results. Specifically, the lack of access to medical knowledge and education is more pronounced within minority communities. The same study indicated that white parents were more aware of ASD and the process of diagnosis and treatment, leading to earlier diagnoses and better outcomes for their children.

Studies like these also indicate problems within the medical system. The findings from studies like this one are an excellent way to bring to light potential structural racism, implicit bias, and provider bias. Even in cases where racial minority children had equally knowledgeable parents compared to white children, outcomes still varied—implying that the difference lies within the quality of medical care those children received.

Moreover, racially different concerns were noticed among parents, which determined various reasons for parents seeking an evaluation for their children. While white parents were concerned about their children's emotions and behavior, parents of Black and Hispanic children were more concerned about communication issues. Hispanic parents who described a child who refused to make eye contact or would not respond to their name were more likely to receive a diagnosis. One potential explanation for this is that "communication issues" may encompass many other ASD symptoms in the eyes of parents of color. All these perceptions contribute to increased difficulties in families of color receiving an autism diagnosis.

Now that you understand the racial disparities in autism let's move on to why an ASD diagnosis is so important.

5

WHY A DIAGNOSIS IS IMPORTANT

Many people undervalue the importance of an ASD diagnosis. This is because people don't fully understand the benefits of getting a diagnosis, and some people are not sure how to go about getting a diagnosis in the first place. Parents are typically unsure who to contact or where to go to get a diagnosis—no one tells you these things. This enlightening chapter will cover all of this and more.

First, how do you know if you must take your child in for screening? Getting an expert's opinion is suitable if your child displays any signs discussed in the previous chapters. Even if it seems like you can easily explain away the symptoms, it is better to be safe than sorry. I recommend you take your child in for a screening or an expert's opinion, even if your child displays only one or two symptoms.

Remember, the sooner you get your child diagnosed, the better. The method of waiting to see if symptoms get worse, persist, or even go away on their own can cause more harm than good. When you get a diagnosis as early as possible, your child can get the help they need for a better future. As discussed earlier, children learn to mask much better as they grow, which can leave symptoms undetected—especially in females. But if you get an earlier diagnosis, your child has the potential to live their entire life with adequate assistance. This drastically improves their chances of living a happy life.

Remembering some of the difficulties we have discussed throughout the book is essential. We know now that it is harder for girls to get a diagnosis than for boys due to masking, differing symptoms, etc. Similarly, those with fewer support needs who don't struggle as much to be social, behave "appropriately," etc., also struggle to receive diagnoses.

One of the many reasons that prevent someone from getting an ASD diagnosis includes a lack of apparent symptoms. Experts may be wary of performing a screening or diagnosis on children who lack noticeable symptoms; this is because experts are afraid of providing the wrong diagnosis. For some reason, doctors would rather turn a child away with no aid than possibly misdiagnosing them; even though a child can and should be screened again, the initial diagnosis can always be reversed and would allow the child to get help because even if they don't have autism, they can have a speech delay or other conditions. This can lead to many doctors initially turning children away, especially if they are female or "high functioning." As I mentioned in the previous chapter, this was the case for my daughter, my goddaughter, and the other children at my daughter's school. This happens more often than you think, and although it is more common in girls, it also happens to boys.

Getting a diagnosis is crucial for your child's well-being; navigating the world without support will become challenging because the world was not built with autistic children in mind. Instead, your child needs access to the resources available—therapy, medication options, education plans, etc., to help them navigate life smoothly. I suppose you are worried about the stigma of a child diagnosed with autism or how such a diagnosis may impact their life, don't be. Your child can be reevaluated and have the diagnosis removed if symptoms improve or disappear. You shouldn't worry about autism "ruining" your child's life; many successful people are on the spectrum!

In addition, there are some cases of children who have been diagnosed with autism that later in life show improvement with their symptoms, in many cases resulting in an ASD diagnosis removal. When this happens, it can be one of two things; in one scenario, it could be that the child's development, therapies, and treatments have created the perfect outcome, and the symptoms/characteristics of autism are so mild or have disappeared to the point that the child can now adapt to the neurotypical world without assistance that was previously needed. The child might have been misdiagnosed in the second scenario because they showed symptoms/characteristics that would signal ASD. As stated before, having some of the symptoms does not mean the child has autism. But as I also said earlier, it is better to err on the side of caution. I have friends who had children with speech delays, and their child was not autistic, so showing one or a couple of the characteristics of ASD does not automatically mean the child has ASD.

Now that we know that the ASD diagnosis can be reassessed let me emphasize that you shouldn't expect this to be the case for your child. Unfortunately, although this can happen, it is not the norm. Hoping for a miracle will distract you from getting your child the help they need and prevent them from accessing resources that will make their life easier in the long run; autism does not just "go away," and most people have the disorder their entire lives. It is better to have the diagnosis and the accompanying resources than to condemn your child to a life of being misunderstood with no help.

REASONS WHY A DIAGNOSIS IS HELPFUL

There are many reasons that a diagnosis is helpful if you have not been convinced so far. Getting a child who has autism diagnosed is one of the best things that you can do to improve the rest of their life, and yours too. Let's discuss some of the reasons why an autism diagnosis is beneficial.

Access to Needed Support

The first reason that getting an autism diagnosis for your child is particularly important is the improved access to needed support, therapies, and more. As I have mentioned throughout the book, symptoms of autism can sometimes improve. This is the result of hard work alongside support and therapeutic options. Your child has a far better chance of dealing with the turns and pushes of the world if equipped with the right tools.

Furthermore, without a diagnosis, it can be challenging to get access to the support and resources that children with ASD need. As unfortunate as this is, many therapies and resources, such as Individualized Education Plans (IEPs), 504s, and speech and behavioral therapy, are restricted to those with diagnoses. Otherwise, the wait times to access these resources can be immense, spanning multiple months or even years. But with a diagnosis, getting support from various sources can be more accessible. Overall, receiving a diagnosis is a gateway into support programs and resources that will ultimately improve the quality of your child's life.

I have seen children who show more advanced symptoms than my daughter or other kids receiving treatment at the clinic where she attends for speech and occupational therapy. These children don't have a diagnosis, so they are put at the bottom of the list when there is a waiting list. The diagnosed children are at the top of the list, even if their symptoms are milder. This breaks my heart because I know that kids who desperately need help must wait longer due to insurance policies and all the bureaucracy that comes with healthcare. I cannot stress enough the importance of a diagnosis; you don't want your child to be at the bottom of the list!

Better Understanding of Behavior

Another significant benefit that stems from receiving a diagnosis has to do with behavior. When your child gets a diagnosis, you will better understand what behaviors result from autism and why. You will be able to understand your child much more deeply. Fundamentally, this is a good thing because you will be able to interact with your child more empathetically and be equipped to help your child manage behavioral issues that cause significant problems in other aspects of their life. As a result, your child will feel much more comfortable interacting with you, and it will aid in building a trusting relationship with them.

In addition, understanding their behavior and what triggers the behavior will help you arrange accommodations that will be needed in school down the road. You'll be competent at explaining why your child behaves as they do to teachers and school administrators. As parents of autistic children, we must be our children's advocates; they can't advocate for themselves, and no one else will do it for them. This will shield your kid from discrimination or unfair treatment due to their disorder. In turn, school will be a more comfortable place for your child, allowing them to be themselves as much as possible while learning, socializing, and interacting with the world around them. This will make school more enjoyable.

As your child progresses into adulthood, understanding the behavior developed in childhood will be instrumental; they will understand themselves better and how to navigate the troubling world surrounding them—one with certain social norms to follow. So, while this will not "heal" your child, it will effortlessly help you and your child acclimate to the real world.

Realistic Sense of Limitations and Challenges

When you are first told that your child has autism, it is easy to let your mind become cluttered with worries; it is overwhelming and terrifying. Stereotypes from the media and news can easily influence the way we perceive autistic individuals, especially if we have no prior experience interacting with those who have ASD. As a result, you can begin worrying about things your child may encounter—some of which will never happen—and neglect to even think about some of the limitations and challenges they will undoubtedly face. After all, we are not taught to become parents, let alone of a child with autism; you will feel completely lost. There was so much I didn't know when my daughter was diagnosed. There is still much I don't know, but I continue to learn so I can continue to provide the assistance that she needs as her needs change. I decided to write this book because there are things I wish I knew, and I hope to help others avoid some of the mistakes I made. I also want to reassure you that every-thing is going to be OK. I don't want to sell you a fairy tale and tell you everything will be easy. It's not, but it's also not impossible. I don't know everything there is to know about ASD, but neither do the experts. I want to help you become an expert on your child and their needs so you can provide them with the best support. Remember, every child is different, and no one, I mean no one, will know your child better than you will. This path set out for you will sometimes be overwhelming and frustrating, but it will also come with its fair share of rewards.

Once again, I will stress the importance of an early diagnosis. The earlier the diagnosis, the earlier you can prepare for all the limitations and challenges you and your child will face. Being prepared is particularly useful for non-verbal individuals with behavioral challenges or mobility limitations. By being prepared, you both will have time to acclimate to the needs your child will require, and it will help you better equip them to face this world built with neurotypical individuals in mind.

Furthermore, this early preparation helps you remember what is and is not realistic to worry about. While this happens less frequently now, some parents take an autism diagnosis as a reason to shelter their child from the outside world, which can cause more issues later in life. Preparing for concerns that do not exist can also harm your child; therefore, it is essential to have a realistic expectation of the challenges and limitations you and your child will face as you progress through this journey.

When we learned of our daughter's diagnosis, we didn't understand how she would react to the outside world. One of the reasons it was hard to quickly notice the differences in her from neurotypical children was that she was kept sheltered due to the COVID-19 pandemic. Some of the "oddities" in her behavior seemed normal for a child sheltered from the outside world for most of their life. Once we learned that there was a more significant reason for her behavior, our first instinct was to protect her from anything and anyone that could harm her. Before learning of her diagnosis, we planned a trip to Disneyland; this would be her first time there since we could not take her during the shutdown. After learning of her diagnosis, we thought it might be best to hold off exposing her to a big crowd as we didn't know how she would react. However, we changed our minds; we decided that we couldn't shelter her from the world and, at one point or another, she would have to face the real world. We couldn't shelter her forever, and we decided that the earlier we exposed her, the earlier we could figure out what accommodations she would need. So, we decided to go to Disneyland after all. But we couldn't help but worry; maybe she'd be completely overwhelmed, and we would have to leave right away; at least we tried. Perhaps she'll be fine at first, but we will have to leave in a few hours; at least she enjoyed herself for a bit. Or maybe she loves it, and we stay all day. I must confess that this seemed like a long shot. Will she even understand that the characters are the same characters she watches on TV? Does it even matter if she enjoys herself? Will she like the rides, or will they be too scary? We played all these scenarios in our minds. Ultimately, we couldn't get an answer to all these questions unless we went. To our surprise, she had no issues being in a large crowd, loved the rides, and recognized the characters when she saw them. She was so happy when she saw the characters; she started jumping, and her stimming was off the charts because she was delighted. My husband and I got teary-eyed, overwhelmed by her joy and excitement. We realized she could do much more than we gave her credit for. She did require some accommodations; she didn't understand that we had to wait our turn in line, and she also didn't know why she couldn't get on a ride with one open seat; she didn't understand we couldn't go on a ride that was down. We could deal with minor annoyances because she had a blast overall, which opened our eyes to her abilities. We were so scared of what could happen when we considered not taking her and focused on what possible inabilities she might experience and not on her abilities. By not taking her, we would have limited her experiences, and she probably would have developed discomfort around big crowds if we had kept her sheltered for too long.

Now, let's dive back into other reasons why a diagnosis is essential.

Academic Benefits

In some sense, it is never too late to get a diagnosis. Your child can receive a diagnosis at any point in their life. But there is something to be said for your child receiving a diagnosis as early as possible regarding academics. Getting a diagnosis before your child ever starts school is best. If your child starts school with you knowing what to expect, the teachers will also know what to expect, and everyone will be on the same page. This will make school a pleasant experience for your child.

When it comes to specific disabilities in an academic setting, teachers and other professionals in your child's school must be aware of their disability. If your child's disability is not disclosed, then your child's school cannot provide reasonable accommodations for your child to succeed. But when your child's school is aware of the limitations and challenges your child faces, they can make appropriate arrangements to help your child excel within that academic environment.

Additionally, your child's disorder being known serves to protect them. Unfortunately, some teachers abuse their power to mistreat children who "misbehave." If your child has accommodations and the school knows of your child's disorder, it protects them from mistreatment and abuse. While you should not have to rely on this to keep your child safe, you can never be too careful.

Establishing an Individualized Education Plan (IEP), 504s, etc., will make life easier for everyone and make your child's school experience much more pleasant and manageable. It is easy for people to judge behavioral problems as the child being bratty. Still, if they understand that the child is triggered by specific sounds, smells, sensory overload, etc., it will be easier to prevent them from being exposed to certain situations. It can avoid a behavioral issue altogether or allow the person in charge of their care at the time to understand why your child is behaving the way they are. The proper actions can be taken to calm the child down, and they can learn to avoid exposing the child to a similar situation.

You can also discuss special education, therapies, transportation, and other services the school district provides for children with ASD and other disabilities. Remember that you must advocate for your child every step of the way; the school districts have so many children to worry about they might not be aware of the needs and accommodations your child needs. Don't be afraid to speak up, ask questions, etc. If your child attends a private school, they, too, will make accommodations. In my experience, I have learned that most people act in good faith and are willing to provide reasonable accommodations if you ask. We have had good experiences with both public and private schools. The main difference is that public schools must provide services and accommodations to kids with disabilities (because they are using our tax dollars), while private schools are not required to. In my experience thus far, the private schools were willing to provide accommodations because they are acting in good faith and looking for a diverse student body.

Financial Support

Financial support is another big reason to get your child diagnosed. There are a few different aspects of financial support that come along with an ASD diagnosis. First, government agencies and other systems will likely offer free or reduced-cost services to children with an official diagnosis. This is especially true when the child is under three years old. This can lower the cost of therapy, counseling, stim toys, and other support items that can improve the quality of your child's life.

The second aspect involves insurance coverage. Insurance covers therapy but, in most cases, only with a formal diagnosis. This is because treatments are considered elective procedures when there is no diagnosis; with a diagnosis, these same procedures are considered a need.

While this financial support might not seem like much initially, it builds up over time. You can save hundreds or thousands of dollars with the financial backing and coverage a diagnosis provides. Most children will need therapy for a few years, and some might need treatment into adulthood.

Another form of financial support your child may qualify for is Supplemental Security Income (SSI). SSI financially supports low-income families with children with developmental and behavioral disabilities. It can benefit a family where one parent must stay home to care for the child. Depending on therapies, school, etc., it becomes difficult for some parents to maintain a traditional job. This is especially true in states where a child's disability does not provide accommodation at work for a parent who has a child with a disability. If you are in a situation where you feel that your job is in jeopardy due to your commitment to your child's care, research the laws regarding parents in your state. Some states have friendly laws for parents to accommodate the needs of their children, while some states only require accommodation for individuals with a disability.

In sum, the access to support, a better understanding of your child and the challenges they will face, having a realistic sense of their limitations, and the academic and financial benefits are well worth getting your child screened for autism. An ASD diagnosis will benefit the entire family in the long run.

DIAGNOSTIC INFORMATION

Who Can Diagnose Autism?

Not every medical practitioner can diagnose autism. It is essential to know who can and cannot diagnose autism—this will save you time and money.

One group of medical professionals who can diagnose autism is developmental pediatricians. Sometimes, these medical practitioners are referred to as developmental-behavioral pediatricians. Developmental pediatricians undergo training and experience related to autism and other developmental issues. They undergo four years of medical school, a specialization and certification in pediatrics, and further training in development and behavior. These doctors are qualified to look for speech and motor skill delays, learning disabilities, developmental disabilities, habit disorders, attention-deficit/hyperactivity disorder, and autism.

Child psychologists are another set of professionals with the necessary tools to diagnose ASD. Child psychologists specialize in children's emotional, social, and mental development, often observing children from birth through adolescence. There are three groups of child psychologists—developmental, youth, and abnormal child psychology. Child psychologists must undergo rigorous training to earn their titles. All child psychologists have the experience to diagnose many disorders, including autism.

Another group of professionals able to diagnose ASD are child psychiatrists, different from child psychologists. Child psychiatrists are specialists in behavioral disorders in children, and the main thing that sets them apart from child psychologists is that a child psychiatrist can prescribe medication, while most child psychologists cannot. Child psychiatrists can also create a specialized treatment plan for your child, including medicine, behavioral therapy, or both.

The final group that can diagnose autism in a child is pediatric neurologists. Pediatric neurologists are doctors who specialize in treating children with issues in the nervous system, which can often cause developmental delays. Because autism is a neurological disorder that affects the brain, neurologists are equipped to diagnose autism in children.

Screening Recommendations

According to the CDC's (2022) screening guidelines, there are a few recommendations that you should keep in mind when it comes to having your child screened for autism. Did you know that autism can be diagnosed earlier than 18 months? I did not know this before either; it is essential to understand the screening recommendations for ASD.

The sooner your child is diagnosed, the sooner treatment becomes available. According to the CDC and the American Academy of Pediatrics, children should be screened for all developmental delays and disabilities—including autism—at nine months old, 18 months old, and 30 months. Additional screening may be needed if your child was born prematurely or with a low birth weight. Your child should also undergo ASD-specific screenings at 18 and 24 months.

It might seem like a lot, but these screenings are essential because ASD symptoms can appear at any stage in life, but quite often, the initial signs are there before a child turns 18 months. As I mentioned before, my daughter's stimming started before she turned 12 months old.

Diagnosis of ASD in children two years old and younger is quite reliable, and it is not a bad idea to take your child in for these regular screenings, even if no risk factors or symptoms are present. And if you do have some concerns, make sure you express them to the doctors. In addition, make sure the doctors focus on what your child is *not* doing instead of what your child is doing.

Seeking a Second Opinion

I am a firm believer in second opinions when it comes to medical issues. Often, what an initial examiner misses, a second practitioner might. If you suspect your child may be autistic, yet your primary doctor has refused a diagnosis, seek a second opinion! Remember that the pediatrician and three different neurologists thought my daughter did not have autism. A lot of doctors are hesitant to diagnose autism for a myriad of reasons, including stigma and bias. This means that some professionals will go as far as denying a child who is autistic from getting a diagnosis due to thinking they are doing you and your family a favor; trust me, they are not!

If you feel like this is what is happening with your doctor, you may need to seek external help to stand up for yourself and your child. Local advocacy groups are available that will help you fight for your child's right to adequate healthcare. Every state within the United States has advocacy groups that help get equal rights for children with disabilities—even if you only suspect the presence of one. Moreover, private and non-profit organizations will support your family through this endeavor, helping you advocate for your child's care. There are also state-funded services to help.

The bottom line is that if you as a parent have the slightest suspicion that your child is autistic—even if it is just a hunch or a feeling that something is off—you should take your child to get screened. The younger your child is when they begin to receive support, the sooner their progress will show.

TYPES OF THERAPIES FOR AUTISM

You should be aware of your child's many options for ASD treatment. Some treatments may work better for your child; work with the healthcare professional who diagnosed your child to find the best treatment options. Empowering yourself with the knowledge of the options available is a great way to ensure that your child thrives. In some cases, therapies alone will provide the support your child needs. In some cases, your child might need medication. Remember that every child is different, and treatment will vary per child. I am not against medication; however, I am hesitant when you walk into a doctor's office and they are ready to provide a prescription before you explain the symptoms.

I've heard testimonials from parents who say food coloring (especially red) exacerbates their child's behavioral difficulties. Parents will remove any foods with food coloring from the child's diet, and they have seen a significant improvement in their child's behavior. I am not saying this is the case for everyone, but getting to know your child and learning what affects them and how is best. I am not against medication, but in my case, I always try to find natural alternatives to fix an issue; if that doesn't work, then I turn to medicine. You need to understand your child, their challenges, and their triggers so you can make the best decision for them.

Applied Behavior Analysis (ABA) Therapy

ABA is a somewhat controversial form of therapy for autism. Before understanding the controversy, we must first understand what ABA is.

ABA is a therapy intended to help children on the spectrum learn skills and lessen problematic behaviors—such as impulsively harming themselves or others. There are many different forms of ABA, and while it has proven effective, some argue that highlighting certain behaviors only helps kids to repeat those behaviors. Many parents and adults with ASD do not support this form of therapy.

One reason that some do not support ABA is because, in its earliest form, it utilized punishment in tandem with reward. While discipline is no longer used in ABA, those who have experienced it first- and second-hand think that the repetitive nature of ABA is too harsh on children. On the other hand, some believe that modern ABA is less repetitive and, therefore, more fun for children, keeping their learning interesting.

It is also argued that ABA is too focused on eliminating behaviors rather than building up other, more valuable skills. Even people who support ABA to an extent agree that this can potentially be problematic, conceding that therapy should focus on what patients should be doing instead of what they should not do. Furthermore, ABA discouraging certain behaviors can be controversial since it can strip some personality-based traits away from children, which leads to my next and final point regarding this controversy.

The last primary reason that ABA is discouraged, especially by those who have autism themselves, is because they believe that ABA tries too hard to make children with autism conform to neurotypical standards. According to opponents of ABA, autistic children have different support needs; therefore, teaching them to act like neurotypical children is wrong. ABA encourages masking-like behaviors, which can ultimately harm a child, and they feel that other forms of therapy would be more helpful overall.

The decision to embark upon ABA with your child is yours and yours only. Although ABA is a controversial method, many revisions have been made to the treatment plan, making it less restrictive. Still, just as is the case with anything else, every child will respond differently. It might benefit your child, or it may not. Ultimately, you decide, get all the information you can, and base your decision on what is best for your child. I have met parents on both sides of the spectrum. The ones in favor of ABA can't imagine what their child would be like without ABA. In contrast, the parents who are entirely against it say it is the worst thing someone can put their child through. Ultimately, you can try it, and if you decide it is unsuitable for your child, you can end the treatment. If you disagree, no one can force you to continue.

In my case, I am not equipped to give a formal opinion because my daughter was affected by the backlog caused by the pandemic and has been on the waiting list to receive ABA since. I decided to try it because I saw the benefits my goddaughter experienced with ABA. Although my daughter has not started the treatment, she has been assessed, and we like that her treatment plan goes hand in hand with the goals and objectives established by her speech and occupational therapy team. This way, we all can work cohesively towards the same goals. Only time will tell if this is a good option for my daughter.

Relationship Development Intervention Therapy

Another type of therapy for autism is called Relationship Development Intervention therapy, or RDI. In RDI therapy, children with autism are taught to bond properly with their parents and extended family members. Flexible thinking, socialization, and introductory psychology skills are introduced to a child who undergoes RDI. Your child will also be taught to adapt to change more effectively. Children with autism struggle to transition from one thing to another; they will learn to master this critical skill with RDI.

As a part of the RDI program, your participation is instrumental. Parents are advised on how to be their child's primary therapist during RDI, which means you will play a vital role in your child's progress. If this is not something you are comfortable with, then RDI therapy might not be for your family; however, if bonding with family comprises the primary struggle of your child, it's worth a try.

Play Therapy

Play therapy for autism will be different than play therapy for other things. When it comes to play therapy for autism, it is far more descriptive than other forms of play therapy. Play therapy is beneficial for autistic children who struggle to interact with others. By utilizing something that comes naturally to children—play therapy enables children to improve their socialization and cooperation skills. Since autism impacts how children interact with other children, play therapy allows children with autism to widen their focus from how they usually play to focusing on how other children play. It can help a child discover new experiences and ways to play, helping them explore their surroundings, emotions, and relationships.

Equestrian Therapy

Equestrian therapy involves horseback riding in an incredibly therapeutic way. Children with autism can ride horses in a completely safe and controlled environment; the therapist is responsible for both the horse's and your child's safety. It has been demonstrated that horseback riding is helpful for communication and social skills and can also reduce irritability and agitation in those who engage in it.

This may be a good option if your child is comfortable around large animals. Socializing with animals can be very therapeutic, and the added benefit of communication with a licensed therapist is terrific. In addition, your child has the potential to pick up a new skill or hobby.

Speech Therapy

According to some, speech therapy is admittedly not the best strategy for many cases of autism (*Types of therapy*, 2022). While many patients do benefit from speech therapy, those with severe autism may be entirely unable to participate. As such, speech therapy will be the most beneficial for those on the lower end of the spectrum. If you are not sure where your child falls in the spectrum or if they could benefit from speech therapy, ask the doctor or doctors guiding you with the treatment plan. Speech therapy is excellent at helping children and adults with autism overcome communication issues and social isolation. However, if you feel your child will not benefit from this option, don't put them through it, as it is time and effort that could be spent elsewhere that can significantly impact your child's well-being.

Cognitive Behavioral Therapy

Cognitive behavioral therapy (CBT) is one of the most popular types of talk therapy to date. CBT includes several sessions for a couple of months, and the primary purpose of CBT is to equip patients with the skills necessary to overcome anxiety and similar side effects of their autism. CBT is beneficial if your child is verbal and can converse fluently. As always, consult a professional if you are unsure if this will be a good option for your child.

Music Therapy

Music is a fabulous tool that can be used to help people with autism relate to their emotions, and it can also help them develop empathy for others. Music therapy entails listening to music, which can help enhance the emotional connection that your child has with themselves and others. If your child is particularly fond of music or struggles with empathy and emotional connection, you might want to try music therapy.

Sensory Integration

Finally, we have sensory integration. ASD is known to impact how those with the disorder perceive sensory input. This can often result in over-stimulation or under-stimulation, proving problematic for a child. Sensory input can be troubling for autistic children, but it can become much easier with sensory integration therapy. Sensory integration involves using sensory information in a controlled environment to help those with ASD manage overwhelming feelings.

THERAPY WAITING LISTS

It is essential to identify the proper form of therapy for your child. Once you do, scheduling a consultation as soon as possible is a good idea, as the waiting lists can be brutal. During the COVID-19 pandemic, this problem only worsened; waiting lists grew longer due to service interruptions. Therapists and children fell ill, slowing down the process and the graduation time, leading to longer waitlists.

While this might not be a big problem now, getting your child on the waitlist as soon as possible is a good idea. Sometimes, it can take a year or longer for a child to receive services, and as we have discussed, the sooner therapeutic intervention happens, the better off your child will be. I know someone who waited three years for ABA therapy; different factors play a role in waiting lists, but the sooner you get on the list, the better.

I also want to point out that just as not all therapies described previously will be the right fit for your child, there will also be therapists that will not be the right fit for your child. You control who provides services for your child, and you don't have to settle. If you feel that a therapist is not the right fit for your child, let the provider know so they can find someone else, speak up! You don't want to waste time with a therapist not helping your child's progress. Sometimes, the incompatibility is due to personality; sometimes, it can be due to the therapist having little experience. Whatever the case is, if you feel your child would benefit from working with a different therapist, request another therapist. We have had to do this a couple of times, and we noticed the difference right away; the bond between a therapist and the child is crucial.

WHAT PROGRESS LOOKS LIKE

Understanding that progress will sometimes look different, even with therapy and all the support you provide your child, is crucial. Sometimes, your child's progress will show leaps and bounds. Other times, their progress will be stagnant. And in some cases, it might even seem that your child is regressing. This happens sometimes when a child is absorbing what they are learning but are not ready to implement it into their everyday lives. Your child's progress curve will not always be on an upward slope; it will have ups and downs. Be patient and try not to set a timeline for your child to reach certain milestones. As parents, we want things to progress a certain way because certain milestones will make life easier for our child, but placing those expectations can be stressful for you and your child. Remember to celebrate every little win because those little victories combined will create a significant impact.

If you take anything from this chapter, it should be that getting a diagnosis as fast as possible is of the essence. I know first-hand that an ASD diagnosis is daunting and comes with many troubling emotions, but the better prepared you are, the better off you and your child will be.

6

DEALING WITH THE EMOTIONS OF AN ASD DIAGNOSIS AND UNDERSTANDING THAT IT IS NOT YOUR FAULT

Being diagnosed with autism will be hard for your child but also extremely hard on you. Acknowledging how your child's disorder makes you feel—especially at the beginning—is nothing to feel guilty about, and it doesn't mean you are making the situation about yourself. It is essential to recognize and deal with your feelings so that they do not tear away at you or damage the beautiful relationship you can have with your child. As we delve into this chapter, we'll talk about how your child's ASD diagnosis may make you feel and discuss ways to help you respond to those feelings.

A lot of fear and uncertainty comes along with the diagnosis of a disability. It can be easy to blame yourself for causing it in some way—this is almost an instinct we have as parents. Finding out that your child has a disability is never easy, regardless of the type of disability, but there are healthy ways to direct your feelings. It is essential to value how you feel and note it rather than suppress it; emotional suppression may negatively impact you and your child, harming your bond. Instead, learning to cope with your feelings and understanding that this diagnosis is not your fault is crucial.

You must understand with certainty that your child's autism is not your fault; you have done nothing wrong. While the causes of autism are unclear to a certain point, as I mentioned earlier in the book, we know one thing for sure: Parenting has nothing to do with your child developing autism. If your child has autism, it is undoubtedly unrelated to anything you have or have not done as a parent. Autism occurs because of factors outside our control, and you played no role in your child's disability. Rest assured that it is not a reflection of you as a parent. You are probably feeling a lot of conflicting emotions right now.

EMOTIONS THAT COME ALONG WITH AN ASD DIAGNOSIS

For every parent, their child's diagnosis comes with an array of emotions. Some parents are relieved, while others are shocked. It is also not uncommon for parents to mourn the life they thought their child would have.

Many parents are relieved because a diagnosis enables them to put a name to what is different or off about their child, giving them a marker to begin helping their child. A diagnosis can often relieve a sense of guilt for parents when they realize that their child's developmental delays have nothing to do with their parenting.

I also know some parents who have felt relief when their child was diagnosed because they know that the diagnosis—just the mere presence of a label like ASD—allows their child access to support and services throughout their life that can make things far more manageable. In other cases, parents did the research, were expecting the diagnosis, and worked hard to get one. Other parents mourn because they believe their children can't have the life they want them to have. Recognizing and accepting your feelings is essential if you feel guilt, grief, relief, fear, stunned, or anything in between.

The ASD Grief Cycle

You've probably heard about the stages of grief in correlation with someone passing away, but a grief cycle can also accompany an ASD diagnosis. While you might be focusing on how this is impacting your child, it is also essential to take some time to focus on how their diagnosis is affecting you. After all, as a parent, you are your child's first teacher. Without your level-headed guidance and ability to make judgments, your child may find themselves lost and without support. Understanding the ASD grief cycle and how it impacts you is crucial to caring for yourself and providing your child with the support they need.

The autism grief cycle begins with shock and disbelief, these are often the first reactions a parent will have upon learning that their child has been diagnosed with autism. Even for parents who suspected a potential diagnosis would occur, disbelief can still cloud one's mind because a diagnosis of any disability is severe, no matter how much you prepared for it. Many parents feel like the impossible is happening or that a mistake was made, which stems from the fact that, at this point, parents usually can't process the full implications of what they have been told. A diagnosis is life-altering, no matter how prepared you think you are. Often, parents who hear the news about their child's autism will go into auto-pilot mode, unable to take in any more information. Some parents feel physical pain, suffocation, or other physical grief indicators.

In my case, I felt my heart sink; I started shaking. I couldn't believe it; I was in complete shock and kept thinking I was having a bad dream I had to wake up from.

If you are a parent encountering the shock and disbelief stage—or if you want to prepare for its potential arrival—there are some things that you can do. For instance, the initial diagnosis will be revealed during a meeting, which you can leave anytime. If you feel overwhelmed and can't handle the news, leave and try to process your feelings. Do not make any decisions until you are done reacting; set up a later appointment once you've had a few days to process the information. It is difficult to process something like this; take all the time you need. In the time between the initial appointment and the follow-up, write down any questions, and make sure you bring them with you.

The next stage is going to be the denial stage. In the denial stage, a parent will usually believe that some mistake has been made and will be cleared up in due time. They feel that their child can't possibly be autistic. And therefore, they struggle to come to terms with the diagnosis immediately. Even in the presence of undeniable evidence, a parent in denial won't overcome the feeling that the results were somehow wrong. Some parents seek second or third opinions to try to clear up this misunderstanding, while others look for some magical cure to alleviate their child's condition.

I remembered the four doctors who agreed that my daughter was not autistic. Maybe they were right? and the psychologist who diagnosed her was wrong; after all, my daughter had more visits with the other doctors. The psychologist only saw her once, there must be a mistake, this can't be real! Even though, at some level, we suspected autism, we were not prepared to hear that autism was a reality in our daughter's life.

The best thing you can do in this stage is reformat your denial to use it positively. Use this time as an opportunity to learn as much about autism as you can, covering many things beyond what this book can ever explain. Research things based on your child's current age and the developmental stages they will be entering. Understand that while you may feel tempted to shop for services and try to find the perfect cure for your child's autism, there is no cure or magical method to make it disappear. Instead, utilize your denial to equip yourself with knowledge to learn more about this disorder.

As I started researching, I was listening to a podcast about autism one day on my way to work. The guest on that episode was a young lady with autism speaking of her experience and how she has processed sensory overload since she was a little girl. She started describing everything she used to do and how she handles it now; it hit me then. She said one specific thing that she did. I can't even remember what that particular thing was, but I said to myself, "Oh my god, my daughter does that exact thing," then I realized that I had to accept that my daughter had autism. It just hit me at that moment, like a bucket of iced water. I cried the entire drive to work, but I knew then that I couldn't deny that my daughter was autistic any longer.

Anger or rage may come next. After the denial stage has diminished, parents usually feel angry. Typical thoughts of parents in turmoil include "Why me?" "Why did this happen to my child when I deeply cared for them? Yet other parents have neurotypical children, and they don't even care for them properly?" In a diagnostic setting, the healthcare provider often breaks the news and bears the brunt of a parent's rage. Parents often yell at the doctor, their partner, the child, and even their sibling(s). Please don't do this! It is normal to feel angry at the mere existence of autism, but it is not OK to take it out on others.

I advise allowing yourself to feel angry but not taking it out on people trying to help you. While people like medical providers are trained to deal with parental anger, that does not mean they deserve it. You have the right to be angry, but that right should not get in the way of the lives of people trying to help you. Instead, understand that anger is a very energetic feeling, and along with the sense of anger often comes the ability to be a positive advocate for your child. As such, you can use your anger to do something positive, such as writing letters to officials overseeing your child's services. If you decide to go this route, wait a few days to send those letters off; read them a few days later to ensure an appropriate tone.

The next feeling that comes in the autism grief cycle is one of confusion and powerlessness. Once the shock, anger, and other initial emotions disappear, you realize you are entering a world you know nothing about. It is like entering another country without knowing their native language—confusing, disheartening, and even scary. You might be worried about the implications of this on your child, and you probably won't understand some of the doctors' terms and instructions. This can make you feel like you must rely on the advice of others, trusting that their expertise will guide you. Sure, the doctor has a degree that says they are reliable, but at the end of the day, they don't know your child like you do.

It is typical to feel confused and powerless because you have just entered a situation entirely foreign to you. However, there is something you can do to regain a sense of power. Use this as an opportunity to begin learning the terminology and the phrases surrounding ASD, and over time; you won't feel so powerless. You will start to feel empowered! With this knowledge, everything will feel more under control, and before you know it, you will be able to make informed decisions independently.

The last stage in the autism grief cycle may be depression. While not everyone enters this stage, it is good to know what to expect and to be prepared if you do. Sometimes, when you have a child on the spectrum, everything can seem like a struggle. These inward struggles will try to devise a solution or cure for your child's disorder, and when no cure comes up, it will lead to feelings of despair. You might feel this is not the life of your dreams, and it is not what you wanted, nor is it what you expected. Being confronted with the realization that your child has a disability can be overwhelming.

If this is the most pervasive feeling in your life, you need to take care of yourself. Admittedly, caring for yourself when you have a child with autism can be quite a feat. Try to get away, even if it's only 30 minutes, and take some time to engage in self-care. It might initially feel selfish, but over time, you will learn the value of self-care and how it makes you a better parent overall.

SEEKING COUNSELING

Raising a child on the spectrum can be simultaneously rewarding and challenging, perplexing us as parents. As you navigate parenting a child with autism and work through the ASD grief cycle, seeking other forms of support may be necessary.

Counseling is an invaluable tool, yet it is also one that many people shy away from. You see, a certain stigma surrounds the idea of counseling. It makes people seeking counseling feel like something is wrong with them. After all, isn't counseling only for people with a problem? And you don't have a problem, right?

There is no shame in seeking counseling. Even though you are not the one who has been diagnosed with ASD, autism still impacts you directly. Seeking counseling for yourself is essential if ASD is causing stress, disappointment, or other strong emotions. But you might be wondering what the benefits of counseling are. Is it really that beneficial?

Well, it is! There are so many benefits to seeking counseling. For example, counseling can help you adjust to the diagnosis. As was discussed in the ASD grief cycle, an autism diagnosis can be traumatic for parents, even if your child is on the lower end of the spectrum. The process for your child to get a diagnosis can be harrowing and take over a year. Multiple visits to myriad professionals over a year or longer can be tiring, and the process provokes many feelings in us as parents. All these feelings can make planning and thinking about the future challenging. An unreal amount of waiting is involved, making everything even harder. Many parents also get told that their child does not qualify for a diagnosis, which means that after a year or two of waiting and suffering, many parents are left with no answers.

The diagnosis can be traumatizing, but so can the lack thereof. Fortunately, understanding the ASD grief cycle can be especially helpful. People have different responses to grief, and some need therapeutic assistance to get through it. Cognitive structuring, cognitive behavioral therapy, eye movement desensitization, reprocessing therapy, and other forms of treatment offered by licensed counselors can help parents overcome the shock of the diagnosis.

Parenting skills are another to consider. You are a great parent if you take this opportunity to learn more about your child and how to help them. But a great parent can always brush up on their skills, and counseling can boost your parenting skills. Parenting a child on the spectrum can differ from parenting a neurotypical child. There are a lot of sensory issues to consider, academic planning to bear in mind, medical needs, safety needs, and so much more. All these responsibilities can be discouraging at times.

As a parent, it is easy to become overwhelmed, and confusion is unavoidable. As crucial as therapy is for your child, it is also essential for you! A counselor knowledgeable in ASD will understand the needs of a family with a child on the spectrum. Having a few sessions with a professional can help you navigate these situations more clearly, cutting down on anxiety and fear when dealing with everything related to your child.

Another thing to keep in mind is how well you connect with your partner. This can be rather difficult when your child has been diagnosed with autism, but it is another way that counseling can benefit you. Studies indicate that parents of children with autism are more likely to struggle with marital problems and divorce rates (Herskovitz, 2015). I'm not surprised by this statistic because relationships are complex, to begin with, and the additional struggles that parents deal with when adjusting to the ASD diagnosis can be very stressful, making an intimate relationship even harder.

Keep in mind that autism is not going to ruin your relationship. Still, how you and your partner respond might systematically tear away at the foundations of your relationship. One of the things to note is that autism magnifies other issues that already exist in a relationship. A counselor will understand your enduring stress and can play a vital role in keeping your family whole while navigating this tumultuous time. Remember that the benefits of therapy do not apply overnight; you need to give it time to work.

Another significant benefit of counseling that helps parents cope with their child's ASD diagnosis is stress management. Stress can be bad enough to make you feel physically unwell, and stress levels are at an all-time high when it comes to coping with a new diagnosis in the family. It is vital to learn effective stress management techniques; a trained counselor can help by providing support, validation, and advice. A counselor can also encourage self-care skills and other stress management techniques that make navigating life much easier.

Remember that, as you navigate your journey, you can't support your child and the rest of your family if you do not have the resources to help yourself first. Parenting is challenging, and parenting a child with autism presents unique struggles that only parents of autistic children can understand. But with the help of a therapist or counselor, you can empower yourself to better care for yourself and your child.

OTHER FORMS OF SUPPORT

A therapist can help you process the struggles with your child's ASD diagnosis, but there are other ways to get support. You can get support from the world around you, including those close to you. People in our immediate circle have a good way of reminding us that despite all the struggles, we still have good reasons to continue living life to the fullest. Other forms of support include support groups, online resources, engaging in self-care, etc. You have plenty of options to care for yourself; becoming the best version of yourself is the best way to help your child and your family.

Family and friends can be the first place to find support. Family and friends are always there for you, and the best part is that they love you and are always willing to lend a helping hand. While your family and friends may not fully understand everything you're going through, they are ready to help in any way they can. Some of your friends might have first-hand experience with autism that they have never shared, making them an excellent support system. Talk to your friends and family about your child's diagnosis—when you feel ready. Kindly ask for their help as you navigate this troubling time. Be specific about how they can help you —this will help them know how to support you more effectively.

Local groups are also great support systems. You will be able to find many support groups in your area specifically geared toward helping parents of autistic children. Support groups offer a safe place for parents to connect, share experiences and advice, or just a shoulder to lean on as they navigate this experience. You can find support groups in your area by looking up "ASD support group near me" or visiting local bulletins. Your doctor or your child's doctor may also be able to recommend a local support group.

Online support is also a great option, especially in smaller towns. Online support groups can help you find online resources and offer advice and support from people with similar experiences. Popular resources that are particularly helpful include The National Autistic Society, The Autism Self Advocacy Network, ABA Mom Blogs, Forums for Parents of Children with ASD, parenting groups on Facebook, and there is also Autism Speaks.

Autism Speaks has come under fire because some people feel that they emphasize the negative aspects of autism and advocate for the need for a cure—and some people feel that autism should be embraced. I like to focus on the positive side of things, present the facts, and allow people to make an educated decision when supporting or doing something. It is also going to be different for different people. A parent with a child on the lower end of the spectrum might feel that their child does not need a cure because they can navigate life with little support. In contrast, a parent with a child on the higher end of the spectrum might feel that a cure would be an excellent solution for their child. Neither parent is wrong; they only want what's best for their child. I think one side shouldn't get to decide for the other. If a cure for autism is found, it should be available to those who want it but should not be forced on those who don't.

Other resources to consider are school district-based resources. Your child's school can offer a handful of specific resources; your school district's special education parent-teacher association (PTA) can be a great place to seek help. The special education PTA group can offer support and advice and provide information about programs and services that might benefit you and your family. Administrators, teachers, and other educators in your child's school may also be able to provide you with resources.

In addition, practicing self-care is vital to your journey. As I mentioned earlier, taking care of yourself is the quickest, safest, and most effective route to aid you in supporting yourself and your family. Becoming stressed and overwhelmed is an unavoidable aspect of parenting, but you can avoid it or lessen it by implementing some discipline.

First, ensure you are getting enough rest (I know, I know, easier said than done)! It can be simple to eschew sleeping enough in favor of taking care of your child, but you should make getting enough sleep one of your priorities—even if it means rotating sleep schedules with your partner. Sleep deprivation can easily lead to the same side effects as being drunk, and you would not trust your child with someone who was intoxicated, would you? Exercise is also a good idea; at least a few minutes daily keeps your body and mind in shape. Exercise helps oxygen get to your brain quicker, making you think better and giving you energy as you go about your day. Combining sleep and exercise will ensure you feel great and can care for your child. Even 10 minutes a day can make a world of difference. Take a 10-minute walk, run up and down the stairs for 5 minutes a couple of times a day, and do squats while brushing your teeth. You can add so many quick workouts to your day without disrupting it; look for resources online if you don't know where to start.

Next, it is essential to understand how to manage your stress because stress management is vital to taking care of yourself. Stress can make us feel nauseous, hurt, or just bad overall. It is harder to function during a stressful situation when we are already stressed. Some good ideas include yoga, meditation, and deep breathing exercises. Engaging in mindfulness and similar activities can help you remain focused and relaxed. I recommend taking a few minutes daily to engage in mindfulness practices to keep your body and mind functioning well.

Respite care is another good option that can provide support and ease some of your stress. Respite care allows a caregiver to take your child off your hands for a few hours or days. This might seem like a rather harsh thing to do, but many caregivers for those with disabilities take advantage of respite care. I recommend looking into credible respite care options available to you, especially if you are a solitary caregiver; you can even have a family member get certified to provide respite care for your child. I strongly recommend taking time to do things you enjoy, even if they are not necessarily "productive." Whether it's a night out, reading a book, or even watching TV without interruptions, doing something you love will make you feel much better. This will seem almost impossible at first, as the demands of the diagnosis process will consume your life, but as you start familiarizing yourself with the care that you will need to provide for your child and once you have a set schedule for therapies, school, extracurricular activities, etc., make sure you find a way to squeeze in time for yourself.

Overall, it is essential to take care of yourself as you begin the journey of being your child's primary care-giver. If you do not care for yourself, you can't take care of them. In the next chapter, we will focus on relation-ships that can sometimes stress caregivers.

7

NAVIGATING RELATIONSHIPS AFTER A CHILD IS DIAGNOSED

Navigating relationships after your child has been diagnosed with autism can be one of the trickiest aspects of managing your personal life. Because your child's ASD takes a significant toll on you, it can also take a major toll on your relationships—especially ones that directly involve your child. Whether it is a partner, the child's siblings, or friends and family, managing relationships alongside raising an autistic child can be challenging, especially at the beginning when you begin to adjust your schedule to your child's needs. Building new relationships can also be difficult. Let's look at how you can work toward managing relationships despite having limited time.

YOU AND YOUR PARTNER

As discussed countless times throughout this book, it is easy to feel lost and overwhelmed after learning about your child's disability. Everyone tells you that the beginning of your journey into parenthood is beautiful —where you get to do so much planning and exploring, preparing for your future. However, an autism diagnosis can be blindsiding and can happen to anyone. During this time, you may think you can turn to your partner—in most cases, your child's other parent—and rely on them for support. And in some circumstances, you can. For some parents, an ASD diagnosis brings them closer together, helping them navigate the journey as partners—this road requires cooperation and can provide a thriving relationship for some parents.

Some parents seem to get closer after an ASD diagnosis. They use the diagnosis as an opportunity to get to know each other better and their child. Through an ASD diagnosis, parents can work together and navigate the journey ahead by planning for their children's and their families' needs and making decisions together. A thriving relationship between two parents makes life smoother—you know who's doing what, who can be relied on for specific needs, and where resources will come from. Financial, medical, and academic endeavors are shared between the couple, building up the relationship while empowering their child.

Unfortunately, for other parents, an ASD diagnosis can bring a time of isolation—one that negatively impacts the relationship with their partner and their family.

It's hard to predict how autism will impact your relationship—unless it's rocky already. In these instances, one or both parents might become isolated and detached. Some parents say things would be better if their child were not diagnosed. This usually happens in cases where one parent is open to seeking the diagnosis, but the other is not. The parent who did not want the diagnosis will often blame the parent who did. This is just one of the ways that resentment can build up between a couple. Resentment can come from other issues, including one parent feeling that they provide more care for the child than the other.

Even when no resentment is present, raising a child with ASD can cause other problems in a relationship. Raising a child with autism can cause overwhelm and strain on a relationship, even if either party perpetuates no blame. For example, one major issue that partners face is a profound decrease in parenting efficiency. When both parents are stressed out and possibly depressed, they become burned out, making spending time on their relationship harder. Intimacy decreases because of parental burnout, and bonding with one another becomes even more difficult. In addition, stress and obligations can take over the lives of both parents. The stress and strain of an ASD diagnosis can cause parents to be unable to spend time with one another, and it can also cause heightened anger, frustration, and depression.

There is also a solid financial burden associated with ASD. Testing alone can be a massive financial burden; some children may need medical devices, therapy, etc., which can harm any relationship, primarily if only one parent works and must take the brunt of the cost of treatments. This can also bring feelings of resentment.

All these things can make it very difficult for relationships of parents with autistic children to thrive. The best thing that you can do to minimize the burden of caring for a child with ASD, as well as the impact that it has on your relationship, is to share the workload. It is essential to establish responsibilities and realistic expectations for both parents. Both parents must agree and understand why things are arranged a certain way. For example, suppose one parent works, and the other doesn't. In that case, both parents need to know that the brunt of financial responsibilities will mainly fall on the working parent. It also makes sense to understand that the parent who is not working would play a more prominent role in the child's direct care. Childcare, chores, working a job, drop-offs/pick-ups from school, therapy sessions, etc., should all be discussed to ensure that both parents contribute equally, even if each contributes differently. This might seem inconsequential, mainly if you are used to a relationship where one person works while the other cleans, for instance. However, sharing the burden of all the responsibilities will ensure that no one gets burned out from carrying a heavier load; this will help keep resentment at bay.

The bottom line is that while you should not anticipate that autism will cause problems in your relationship, you should be prepared if it does. By preparing yourself for these possible scenarios, you can take direct action to avoid these things from happening or restore your relationship if they have already happened. Don't forget to use respite care and babysitting to spend time alone with your partner; make sure you plan date nights and other things to do together. Don't hesitate to seek counseling if you feel things are getting worse. All these things will aid in making you better caretakers and better partners. Ensure you utilize all the tools to help you and your family thrive.

IMPACT ON SIBLINGS AND OTHER CHILDREN

You and your partner will not be the only ones whose relationship will be impacted by the diagnosis. The diagnosis will also affect siblings and other children within the family unit. To successfully keep all children in the household happy, you must understand the impact that autism can have on everyone.

Regarding any disability, siblings of children with disabilities face distinctive challenges, and autism is no exception. However, one crucial thing to remember is that every situation is unique. There are a few shared experiences that people who are the siblings of someone on the spectrum will experience almost universally, and you should be aware of them to help your other children navigate these experiences.

One of the things that a sibling of someone with autism may face is ableist embarrassment. It is one of the most complex challenges that siblings face, especially as they approach their middle years in education. The unfortunate aspect of being a child is that children are not as understanding as adults about disabilities—at least not typically. This can lead to loud, public examples of embarrassment that take an ableist connotation. For example, a child may call their autistic sibling a freak or something worse; they might ask their sibling what's wrong with them.

The best thing that you can do is to teach your children to stand up for themselves and their siblings, expressing support for the autistic child, as well as expressing intolerance for ableist behaviors and speech. It is also a good idea to inform your child that they have the right to refuse a child entrance into their home or life if they are going to be ableist toward their sibling.

Resentment is also widespread in the struggles that siblings of children with autism face. A disability diagnosis causes everyone in a family to have to readjust. When this happens, you will want to keep the autistic sibling's feelings and needs at the forefront. However, some parents neglect to consider the mental health issues the child without a disability may suffer. If they feel neglected, it is easy for them to form feelings of resentment toward their autistic sibling. This is because they will have to compromise, adapt, and change to the needs of their autistic sibling. They might feel their needs are never at the forefront of a situation. While one child is disabled, it is essential to remember that your other child is still, in fact, a child. They do not want to sacrifice parts of their childhood for their siblings, no matter how much they love them. These problems compound as kids grow up and realize that parents do not have as much time or money due to the autistic child. This can be rather disheartening, causing them to lash out at their sibling or their parents.

One tactic that can be used to avoid this situation is to carve out specific time to spend with your neurotypical child. For example, after your autistic child goes to bed, consider letting your neurotypical child stay up late (maybe on a weekend). During this time, take time to spend with them watching their favorite movie or doing their favorite activity; make sure the time is all about them. While this will not solve all issues, it will allow them quality, one-on-one time with their mom and dad without sharing the spotlight with their sibling.

The third most significant problem that a sibling of an autistic child will face is greater expectations. When there is a disability in the family, every family member must help support them, which does not exclude siblings. Siblings are often expected to manage their emotions and needs, keep up with more chores, and avoid their hobbies and other things they enjoy to help their autistic siblings—even if they are very young. Even into adulthood, siblings will have to take on more and more responsibility. These greater expectations pushed onto one child can cause issues with their mental health.

It is essential to recognize and address the needs of the non-autistic sibling(s); it can be challenging due to all the time and effort that caring for a disabled child requires. It is also easy to assume that everything is fine with the non-autistic child because we view them as self-reliant. This does not mean that they don't need our time and attention. Just as it is essential to carve out some time for self-care, it is also important to carve out time to spend with your neurotypical child or children; this will prevent feelings of resentment within the family unit.

DEALING WITH FAMILY

You may have family members—usually extended family—who refuse to accept that your child has been diagnosed with autism. There are many reasons for this, and while those reasons do not make it any more valid for them to invalidate your child's diagnosis, understanding their reasons might make it easier for you to understand their point of view while educating them on why it's better for your child that they fully understand their behaviors, triggers, etc.

One of the reasons your family members might deny your child's diagnosis is generational differences. Social media and added awareness have made it so that younger generations know that autism and other disabilities are not rare. More youthful people understand that many have them, and not all are visible. But just a few decades ago, it felt infrequent to see a disabled child and even rarer to see a disabled adult, which perpetuated the idea with older generations that disabilities are uncommon. This can make older people hesitant to accept the diagnosis because it is so rare that it could never happen to someone in their own family —at least in their minds. The farther back you go, the harder it is for generations to accept the prevalence of such disabilities. Educating older generations is tricky, making it hard to break down their idea that autism and other disabilities are sporadic.

In addition, the fear of stigma can prevent some older individuals from acknowledging that a child in their family has autism. To more senior people, autism is considered something bad. It is a disheartening and unfortunate reality, and it is exhausting to have to keep trying to explain to older members of your family what autism is and that ignoring the diagnosis is not helpful to the child. However, they mean well because they are worried about your child being judged. They might also be afraid they will be judged for having someone with a disability in their family. Fortunately, this problem will disappear as the world becomes more conscious of neurodiversity.

Older people in your family might also reject your child's autism diagnosis because they do not understand what ASD is. Some people only know what they've seen in the media and news—most of which is not good. This means they are blind to the disorder's symptoms, implications, and overall nature, causing them to be rather judgmental.

So, what should you do about a family member with an unwavering opinion that your child's autism is not real? If you feel they would be open to it, you can try educating them. Do not go about it by spouting unfamiliar language at them. Remember how you felt when you first learned about your child's autism diagnosis—confused, scared, and alone. This is how someone you are educating may feel as well. The best thing to do is to learn what they know about autism and start the re-education process.

In some cases, some people will not be open to being educated. In these cases, I recommend being honest about your child's struggles but do not talk to them about it in terms of autism. For example, if your child does not like being touched due to their autism, tell them that your child is sensitive to touch by saying, "She doesn't like getting hugs; please respect her personal space." You may get a better response by saying that than "Her autism makes her sensitive to sensory input."

DEALING WITH FRIENDS

Although most of your friends will provide support in many ways, it is during trying times that you find out who your real friends are. Most of your friends will want to educate themselves to be able to understand and support you. Some of your friends might already have some insight into autism, and they can help you by providing guidance. However, just like family members, you will have a friend or two who don't understand disabilities. These so-called friends might offer their support, but you might realize that they no longer want their children to come around your child, or you might notice that they don't come around like they used to.

If you feel the need to educate them, you can do so. Otherwise, cut them out because you don't need the added stress of a fractured relationship. Your time is even more valuable now because the little or almost nonexistent extra time that you have in your life should not be spent doing things or spending time with people that are not adding value to your life.

I know this contradicts the advice on dealing with family, but you shouldn't rush to cut a parent, sibling, cousin, aunt, or uncle out of your life because they have a blood bond with your child. A friend has no such bond to your child, especially if they choose not to come around or distance their children from your child. I am also not completely opposed to cutting out family members; I'm just saying some steps should be taken before doing so. As I have repeatedly stressed throughout this book, you must do what is best for you and your child.

BUILDING NEW RELATIONSHIPS TO CREATE A SUPPORT SYSTEM

As you navigate this time in your life, you may want and *need* to build new relationships to develop the right support system for yourself and your child. You can do this in the following ways:

- Make a list of existing family members, including your extended family. Which members would be likely to help you when it comes to caring for your child? Do you have family members willing to babysit or offer respite care? Or siblings and cousins who can provide you with some time for self-care? Remember, this doesn't have to be a full day; it can be an hour or two. And don't forget about your friends; your true friends will be there for you no matter what and will be willing to help you in any way they can.

- Think about joining a local support group. A local support group is a beautiful way to make friends who know exactly what you're going through. One of the best aspects of a support group for autism is that the people there already understand some of your struggles, making it an empathetic and open place to address your concerns.

- Work closely with your child's teacher(s) at school; working with them to provide the best possible care for your child is a way to ensure your child is receiving optimum care. Teachers are not the only ones willing to help; administrators, librarians, therapists, counselors, and other leaders within the school may be willing and able to offer support.

- Get support for yourself as needed; this can be through therapy, counseling, or self-care such as meditating, yoga, or just making time for an old hobby or starting a new one. Remember that helping yourself will help your child, too, because you will have the patience and clarity to address their needs. Taking care of yourself is not selfish, so don't feel guilty. Take advantage of the resources that are available to you so you can help your child succeed.

- If you find it difficult to process your child's diagnosis, consider enrolling in parent training to find supportive individuals who can make the journey easier. The National Center for Parent Information and Resources is a great place to find parent training for each state within the United States, offering state-funded programs.

- Research the available community resources. Many communities—especially in bigger cities—offer various activities and resources for families that can help keep kids active, provide parents with resources, and otherwise offer support to ensure you and your child don't feel alone. Research the available resources in your area.

- You can also check online resources. Many online support groups offer free or cost-effective training courses and information that make it easier to parent your child.

- You can also look to your colleagues for support. It can seem natural to keep your work life separate from your home life, but some benefits are associated with asking your boss and colleagues for help or just making them aware of your situation. By knowing your case, your boss and colleagues can be more empathetic when you need to request time off or if you need to have more flexibility with your work schedule. If you feel they will be supportive, let them know what you are going through, so they understand that you are not slacking off when you request to leave early or request time off.

- There are many ways to find support in your community when raising an autistic child. Remember that it takes a village to raise a child —even one without a disability—and there is nothing wrong with looking to those around you for support.

It is a long, hard road, but you can have successful relationships if you don't let ASD control your life. In the beginning, it will seem as though ASD controls every moment and every aspect of your life, but as you start to pile on your support systems, things will begin to seem more manageable. You can create a schedule to accommodate all your family's responsibilities. With your newfound knowledge, you can maintain strong and fulfilling relationships with the people already in your life and the new people who are ready to welcome you into their lives.

Take a Moment to Help Another Parent

You're ready to help your child thrive … and that means you're also ready to help another parent!

Simply by sharing your honest opinion of this book and, if you're happy to, a little about your own experience, you'll help other parents find the peace of mind and guidance they're looking for.

Thank you so much for your support. I wish you and your child nothing but happiness going forward.

Scan the QR code here

CONCLUSION

Being a parent is one of the most beautiful things in the world. You get to take a new being that you helped create or took into your care—as is the case with adoption. And now you have the glorious opportunity to spend your life molding theirs, helping them navigate anything that comes their way. Autism is one of those things that can come their way, and with the right tools, you can help them navigate it.

In this book, you have mastered and unlocked the secrets to truly embracing the autism spectrum. Now, you are an expert in identifying signs indicating that your child may be autistic. You know it may be harder to identify autism if your child is a female or non-white. You also understand the misconceptions and history surrounding autism. You are also educated on the disparities women and people of color face when dealing with autism, why a diagnosis is essential, and how to get one. More importantly, you know how to support your child and yourself during this upsetting time.

Many people feel like having a disabled child is a bad thing. I don't feel that way at all, and now I understand that everything happens for a reason; maybe there is a lesson in all this. In my case, it was patience and the opportunity to help others. I had very little patience before my daughter was born. I became more patient when she was a baby, but my patience has grown exponentially after her diagnosis. I like to recognize my beautiful child for what she is—a gifted and talented little girl who will do amazing things. Believe it or not, the way you think about autism and the perceptions that you have also impact the way that your child feels about themselves. If you treat their differences like the gift they are—something to be celebrated and not shunned—then this is the mentality that your child will have as well. It will carry them through life in a positive way.

Another thing that autism has given me is the ability to celebrate every little thing, things that parents of neurotypical kids might take for granted. It was so exciting when my daughter finally mastered using a spoon. The day she said "I love you, Mommy" for the first time (she was almost five) made me teary-eyed. Whenever she says a new word, when she shows excitement about something, when she connects real life with something she sees on TV. And on and on the list goes; you see, if my daughter were neurotypical, all these things would seem trivial, and I wouldn't be able to see them for the little miracles that they are.

Autism does not have to be something that you dread. I encourage you to embrace the spectrum, continue to educate yourself, and get to know your child as an individual rather than getting to know them through their condition. Remember that ASD is a part of them, but they shouldn't be defined by it. It is only one part of who they are and not who they are entirely.

I also want to reiterate that there will be challenges to face; you will have to become your child's advocate, and at times, you might have to fight fearlessly to get them the support they need, whether it be from the doctors, the school system, the health insurance provider, or any other type of support that they may need. But just as there will be challenges, there will also be a lot of victories, some small, some big. Raising a child on the spectrum is very rewarding; all you have to do is embrace it and remind yourself to take it one day at a time. No one said it would be easy; they just said it would be worth it!

I hope that you have taken many positive things from this book. If you have found this book helpful, please leave a review! That way, other parents like you can access this valuable information.

Now that you have the tools and resources to embrace the spectrum. I hope you will come back to this book when you find yourself in need of guidance or advice. Thank you so much for allowing me to lead you along this journey—get out there and use what you have learned to improve your child's life!

REFERENCES

107 Favorite Quotes About Autism and Aspergers. The Art of Autism. Last modified March 30, 2022. https://the-art-of-autism.com/favorite-quotes-about-autism-and-aspergers/

Autism first signs: A checklist for babies and toddlers. (2022). Autism SA. https://autismsa.org.au/autism-diagnosis/autism-symptoms/signs-of-autism-in-babies/

Autism myths and misconceptions. (n.d.). https://adsd.nv.gov/uploaded Files/adsdnvgov/content/Programs/Autism/ATAP/Autism% 20Myths%20and%20Misconceptions.pdf

Autism Speaks. (n.d.). *Research reveals racial differences in perceptions of autism prior to diagnosis.* https://www.autismspeaks.org/science-news/research-reveals-racial-differences-perceptions-autism-prior-diagnosis

The autism spectrum disorder grief cycle. (n.d.). FamilyEducation. https://www.familyeducation.com/kids/neurodiversity/autism/autism-spectrum-disorder-grief-cycle

Aylward, B. S., Gal-Szabo, D. E., & Taraman, S. (2021). Racial, ethnic, and sociodemographic disparities in diagnosis of children with autism spectrum disorder. *Journal of Developmental & Behavioral Pediatrics, 42*(8), 682-689. https://doi.org/10.1097/dbp.0000000000000996

Bonnello, C. (2016, March 9). *What to do when your family doesn't accept autism.* Autistic Not Weird. https://autisticnotweird.com/family-doesnt-accept/

Centers for Disease Control and Prevention. (2018, April 26). *Spotlight on: Racial and ethnic differences in children identified with autism spectrum disorder (ASD).* Centers for Disease Control and Prevention. https://www.cdc.gov/ncbddd/autism/addm-community-report/differences-in-children.html

Centers for Disease Control and Prevention. (2022, Dec 6). *Screening and Diagnosis of Autism Spectrum Disorder for Healthcare Providers.* https://www.cdc.gov/ncbddd/autism/hcp-screening.html

Centers for Disease Control and Prevention. (2023a). *Data and statistics on autism spectrum disorder.* https://www.cdc.gov/ncbddd/autism/data.html

Centers for Disease Control and Prevention. (2023b). *Signs and symptoms of autism spectrum disorders.* https://www.cdc.gov/ncbddd/autism/signs.html

Child Mind Institute. (2023, Jan 31). *The controversy around ABA.* https://childmind.org/article/controversy-around-applied-behavior-analysis/

Herskovitz, J. (2015, July 14). *4 ways counseling can benefit autism spectrum parents.* GoodTherapy. https://www.goodtherapy.org/blog/4-ways-counseling-can-benefit-autism-spectrum-parents-0714154

LeGare, J. (2022, March 24). *Link between autism and vaccination debunked.* Mayo Clinic Health System. https://www.mayoclinichealthsystem.org/hometown-health/speaking-of-health/autism-vaccine-link-debunked

Novak, S. (2022). *Autism myths and facts.* WebMD. https://www.webmd.com/brain/autism/features/autism-myths-facts

Quick Safety 23: Implicit bias in health care. (n.d.). The Joint Commission. https://www.jointcommission.org/resources/news-and-multimedia/newsletters/newsletters/quick-safety/quick-safety-issue-23-implicit-bias-in-health-care/implicit-bias-in-health-care/

Reasons for and against seeking a diagnosis. (n.d.). Care and Support in Cornwall. https://www.supportincornwall.org.uk/kb5/cornwall/directory/advice.page?id=d3EQRsT_EFg

Rudy, L. J. (2022). *What it's like being the sibling of a child with autism.* Verywell Health. https://www.verywellhealth.com/challenges-of-having-a-sibling-on-the-autism-spectrum-4114557

The Recovery Village. (2022, April 14). *The history of autism.* The Recovery Village Drug and Alcohol Rehab. https://www.therecoveryvillage.com/mental-health/autism/history-of-autism/

Types of therapy for autism: 8 therapies to consider. (2022, Feb 22). Songbird Therapy. https://www.songbirdcare.com/articles/types-of-therapy-for-autism

Who can diagnose autism? (2021, March 9). Therapeutic Pathways. https://www.tpathways.org/faqs/who-can-diagnose-autism/